A Joy
Forever

A thing of beauty is a joy for ever:
Its loveliness increases; it will never
Pass into nothingness; but still will keep
A bower quiet for us, and a sleep
Full of sweet dreams…

– John Keats, *Endymion*

A Joy Forever

MARIE WEBSTER'S QUILT PATTERNS

Rosalind Webster Perry
and Marty Frolli

PRACTICAL PATCHWORK

This book of patterns is dedicated to the memory of their creator
Marie Daugherty Webster
(1859–1956)
who has been our inspiration
just as she has inspired countless others
and to
Jeanette Scott Thurber
her daughter-in-law
who lovingly preserved these quilts and patterns
for the enjoyment of future generations.

Published by
Practical Patchwork
P.O. Box 30065
Santa Barbara, CA 93130
an imprint of Espadaña Press

Printed in Hong Kong

Library of Congress Catalog Card Number: 92-080786

ISBN 0-9620811-7-5

Cover and Frontispiece: *Iris. 82" x 83". Linen and cotton. This quilt was designed and made by Marie Webster in 1910 and was shown in her first feature in the* Ladies' Home Journal, *January 1, 1911. The complex interplay of delicate flowers, straight stems and sword-shaped leaves creates a fascinating pattern. More flowers appear in the quilting along the border and in the center of each block. (Collection of Rosalind Webster Perry.) Pattern begins on page 58.*

Contents

Tissue paper placement guides were included in Marie Webster's pattern packets.

Poppy pattern.
Tissue paper guide for the center medallion.

Iris pattern.
Tissue paper guide for the border.

Preface

This book is a tribute to the creativity and vision of one woman, Marie Daugherty Webster, whose quilt designs have brought beauty and joy to thousands of people over the last 80 years. It is the very first collection of her patterns—the result of a unique collaboration between her granddaughter, Rosalind Webster Perry, and Marty Frolli, an experienced quilt designer and teacher.

History does repeat itself! When color pictures of Marie Webster's quilts were first published in the *Ladies' Home Journal* in 1911, she was immediately besieged by requests for her patterns. Quiltmakers seemed equally enthusiastic in 1990, when Rosalind published a new edition of her grandmother's book, *Quilts: Their Story and How to Make Them*. Once again, letters arrived from quilters all over the country, requesting patterns for these classic designs.

Fortunately, Rosalind had access to a fine collection of original patterns, saved by her mother, Jeanette Thurber, Marie's daughter-in-law. But the directions, written between 1911 and 1930, were extremely brief by today's standards and needed to be adapted. When Rosalind enrolled in a quilting class, she soon realized that her instructor, Marty Frolli, would make the perfect co-author. An inspiring teacher, Marty created all the patterns and hand-outs for her students on her computer.

Rosalind and Marty developed their own method of reproducing these historic designs. First, Rosalind redrew the patterns to eliminate the confusing turn-under allowances on the originals. Next, these drawings were scanned onto computer disks. Then Marty spent countless hours at the computer (when she would rather have been quilting), translating these images into finished art work and writing new directions. Rosalind contributed the essay, "Marie Webster, Quilt Designer," which serves as an introduction to the patterns.

We wish to thank the many people who have helped us, especially Cuesta Benberry, Nancilu Burdick, Jan Hanreddy Freeman, Marilyn Goldman, Elsa Greene, Mrs. Henry Greene, Joyce Gross, Nancy Jacoby, Pat Nickols, Bets Ramsey, Mrs. Paul Thompson, Merikay Waldvogel and the Public Library of Marion, Indiana. Special thanks to our good friend, Zetta Hanna, who made the beautiful Daisy quilt. She was always happy to share her extensive knowledge of quilting and appliqué techniques.

We would like to thank all the owners of the quilts illustrated here, for graciously allowing us to study and photograph their treasures, and also Niloo Paydar of the Indianapolis Museum of Art, for access to the quilts in the Webster Collection.

Finally, thanks to our talented husbands, Mark Frolli and Dick Perry, for their constant encouragement and indispensable advice! Mark patiently answered our numerous questions about computer applications, and Dick designed the cover and assisted with many other facets of book production.

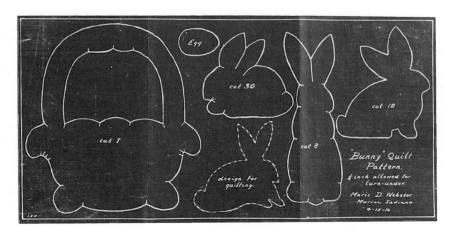

Bunnies pattern blueprint, dated 4-15-16.

Poppy. *92" x 83". Linen and cotton. This was Marie Webster's most influential quilt, for its elegant central design started a revival of the medallion style, which had been popular in the early 1800s. This format was widely copied in the appliqué quilts of the 1920s and 30s. Her initials, MDW, and the date 1909 are quilted on the border. (Private collection.) Pattern begins on page 69.*

Marie Webster, Quilt Designer

Marie Webster's quilts have been favorites ever since they were first published eighty years ago. They are renowned for their elegance and simplicity, reflecting her belief that beauty should be combined with practicality.

I have had the good fortune to live with these quilts all my life. I knew their maker well, for my grandmother lived with us while I was growing up. But it has only been in the past few years that I have started to look at them carefully and wonder what special qualities set them apart and make them universally admired.

Each of her quilts was planned as a unified whole around a single theme, usually a particular kind of flower. By studying the actual blossoms—their shapes, their colors and their patterns of growth—my grandmother was able to capture their essential character through the traditional techniques of hand appliqué and quilting. The perennial appeal of these natural motifs and their harmonious expression in fabric have guaranteed that these designs would become classics.

Marie Webster absorbed many influences from the world around her. At the beginning of the 20th century, new ideas—popularized by the Arts and Crafts movement—were revolutionizing American taste. Those things that had been the most popular in the Victorian era were now the most vigorously rejected. Nature provided artists with fresh themes for their designs and traditional handcrafts were revived.

My grandmother's work was very much in tune with these emerging trends. Insofar as her patterns have changed the direction of quilt design, the effect of the Arts and Crafts movement on quiltmaking has been far-reaching indeed.

Today, we can look back and appreciate just how influential her quilts have been. They sparked the pre-World War I "quilt craze" and grew ever more popular during the Great Quilt Revival of the 1930s. Now, increasing interest in her work makes the publication of these wonderful patterns as timely today as it was in the early years of this century, when they first appeared in print.

Marie Webster's parents

Minerva Lamoreaux Daugherty
(1836–1922)

Josiah Scott Daugherty
(1827–1910)

Marie Webster *(seated, left) with her brothers and sisters— Karl, Lucy, Emma and Lawrence Daugherty. Her husband George, holding their son Lawrence, is seated on the right. Photographed in Wabash, Indiana, in 1889.*

Early Life

My grandmother's roots were firmly planted in the Midwest. Born in northern Indiana in 1859, she lived there almost all of her life. Her own grandparents had come as pioneers to the sparsely settled region before 1850, when a simple rural life style was still the rule. By the time her parents, Minerva and Josiah Daugherty, married in 1858, the forests were giving way to farmland—some of the most productive in the country. Their little hometown of Wabash was growing and life was becoming easier, with manufactured goods arriving, first by canal and later by railroad, from the East Coast and even from Europe.[1]

Marie's father was a major influence in her life. A tall thin man with a long beard and a commanding presence, he was an explorer and rancher as well as a dynamic businessman and civic leader. Marie, like most girls in the 19th century, spent much of her time at her mother's side. As the oldest of six children, she was expected to assume responsibilities beyond her years and assist her mother with a myriad of household chores.

Marie learned to sew at an early age—probably as soon as she was able to hold a

Marie Daugherty at age 4 in 1863

needle. The tiny stitches so characteristic of her quilts must have been perfected by constant practice as a child. Her mother, Minerva, had learned to sew before the introduction of the sewing machine in the 1850s, and she passed on the traditions of both plain and fancy handwork to her three daughters.

To their credit, the Daughertys believed in the importance of a good education for their daughters as well as for their sons. Marie stayed in school and in 1878, she graduated with distinction from high school. However, her aspirations for a college education were thwarted by the allergies that often plagued her during her long life.

She consoled herself by reading everything she could get her hands on, especially novels, history, travel and the classics. Although dedicated to her studies, she was by no means a bookworm. The Daughertys' spacious red brick home was a center of social life in Wabash, where visitors often stopped when traveling through the region. Marie met her future husband, George Webster, Jr., while he was in Wabash on business from the nearby town of Marion, Indiana.

Marie Daugherty at age 10 in 1869

Crazy Quilt

My grandmother made a crazy quilt during her engagement to George Webster, Jr. It is inscribed with the date 1880, four years before her marriage, but is monogrammed with the initials of her married name—MDW.

This is a typical crazy quilt, composed of many blocks of silk and satin scraps. The colorful pieces were sewn onto a foundation and embellished with a delightful array of painted flowers and embroidery stitches.

Many of the same motifs—roses, pansies, daisies, grapes and vines—would also appear on the appliqué quilts she would design some thirty years later. But the colors reflect the taste of the times. Rich reds, dark greens, browns and grays predominate, seasoned with blue, yellow and black.

Like most crazy quilts, this one was not actually quilted. Marie never considered it to be a "real" quilt. It is, however, the only quilt she is known to have made before 1909, when she made her first appliquéd quilt—an event that would change her own life as dramatically as it changed the history of 20th century quilts.

Crazy Quilt detail.
Marie embroidered her monogram—MDW—in one of the blocks, and entwined the red letters with delicate grapevines and clusters of fruit.

Crazy Quilt. *52" x 62". Made by Marie Daugherty Webster, 1880–1884. This spirited rendition of a typical Victorian crazy quilt was pieced in 42 blocks of silk and velvet scraps. Such fancywork was very time consuming—several years could be spent adorning every square inch with multi-colored decorative stitchery and painted flowers. (Private Collection).*

Marie Webster in her quilt lecture costume.

Marie Webster, about 1900.

Emma Daugherty (1866–1952),
Marie's younger sister. Emma made
the French Baskets quilt shown on
page 29 and the May Tulips quilt
on page 32.

Lawrence Webster,
Marie's son, in his
World War I uniform,
1917. Lawrence drew
the blueprints for his
mother's pattern
business.

The Webster Family

Marie Daugherty was a fashionable and witty young woman, with auburn hair and sparkling hazel eyes. She was married to George Webster in Wabash, Indiana, in a romantic Valentine's Day ceremony in 1884.

They spent most of their fifty-four years of married life in George's hometown, Marion. Their only child, a son named Lawrence, kept Marie busy in the early years of their marriage. Her many other interests included reading, sewing and amateur dramatics, as well as a variety of social and volunteer activities.

The discovery of natural gas beneath the town in 1887 triggered a boom which brought the area unparalleled prosperity. Marion was transformed from a quiet county seat into the bustling commercial center of Indiana's "Gas Belt." The very first well was drilled only a few blocks from the Websters' home, and the sound of hissing gas could be heard throughout the neighborhood. The supply seemed inexhaustible and gas lights were left burning day and night along the city streets.

Entrepreneurs soon arrived in Marion to take advantage of the offer of free land and free fuel for their factories. Within a few years, they were producing steel, tin, furniture, paper and glass, including the world famous Mason jar. When George became a partner in a thriving bank, the Webster family prospered along with the rest of the town.

The pace of life quickened. Wealthy business executives built mansions and entertained on a lavish scale. Marie and George enjoyed this active social life, and also traveled extensively, enabling Marie to experience the cultural life of New York, Chicago and Philadelphia.

One of their most memorable trips was in 1893, to the spectacular Columbian Exposition at the Chicago World's Fair. They also made a "grand tour" of Europe in 1899, when England's Arts and Crafts movement and France's Art Nouveau style were at their peak.

In 1902, the Websters moved into a new house at 926 South Washington Street, the principal thoroughfare of Marion. This elegant Colonial Revival building would be their home for the next forty years and would become the center of Marie's quilt pattern business. In the backyard was her beloved flower garden, where she cultivated the irises, poppies, daffodils and tulips which inspired her quilt designs.

The Webster House,
926 South Washington
Street in Marion,
Indiana.

The Arts & Crafts Movement

The beginning of the 20th century was a time of innovation in art and design. Marie Webster's work reflects two important trends in the decorative arts: the Arts and Crafts movement, introduced to the United States from England, and the Colonial Revival, which led to a renewed appreciation of American folk art.

The Arts and Crafts movement was born during the mid-19th century, in response to the stresses of rapid industrialization. William Morris (1834-1896), the visionary designer and social critic, was its spokesman and leader. Reacting against the depersonalization and ugliness of the Industrial Revolution, his work was imbued with nostalgia for the Middle Ages. He longed to escape from the excesses and "depressing materialism" of the Victorian era to recreate a time when beauty could be found in handmade objects. Simplicity, honesty of expression and fidelity to nature were the cornerstones of his philosophy.

Morris was responsible for a revival of all the decorative arts. In his own designs for textiles, wallpaper and carpets, Morris favored plant forms with strong outlines. These bold two-dimensional patterns are still popular today.

After gaining momentum in England, the Arts and Crafts movement swept over America, releasing a great outpouring of creative energy in architecture and the decorative arts.

Traditions of fine handcrafts in ceramics, furniture, glass, metal and book design were revived. Many outstanding designer–craftsmen, working in various styles, expressed a similar concern for the honest use of natural materials and for clean and uncluttered lines. Above all, these artists turned to nature for inspiration.

Louis Comfort Tiffany designed his richly ornamental glass in the popular French Art Nouveau style, while furniture designers like Gustav Stickley developed the plain and sturdy Mission style. Charles and Henry Greene, Louis Sullivan and Frank Lloyd Wright, the most original architects of their generation, were also closely associated with the movement.

Many women were active in the Arts and Crafts movement, finding personal fulfillment and the rare opportunity to earn a "respectable" living. Artists like Jessie Wilcox Smith and Elizabeth Shippen Green became successful illustrators. A number of Art Pottery firms, including Rookwood Pottery and the Newcomb College Pottery, provided women with avenues to serious professional careers.

New magazines, like *House Beautiful* and *House and Garden,* introduced Arts and Crafts ideas to the growing urban and suburban middle class. Simple, clean home interiors replaced fussy and dusty Victorian furnishings. In needlework, elaborate fancywork, like the lavishly embroidered but impractical crazy quilts, went out of fashion.

The Arts and Crafts movement was given an American flavor by the Colonial Revival, which had been growing in popularity since the Philadelphia Centennial Exposition of 1876. This watershed event featured a variety of displays of 18th century life, including a colonial kitchen and examples of needlework and other crafts.

It was not long before people realized that these traditional handcrafts, although extinct in urban areas, were still flourishing in the more isolated parts of the country, which had been spared the effects of industrialization. Schools were set up in the Appalachian mountain region to preserve the traditions of basketry, weaving and woodworking. Folk art designs, like the Pennsylvania Dutch motifs found on country pottery, became fashionable. All of these rural crafts were embraced by the middle class as representing the best of our colonial heritage.

The Colonial Revival also carried a moral message by stressing the values of an idealized time in our nation's history. By reviving the crafts practiced before the Civil War, Americans believed they could also recapture the traditional values eroded by the Industrial Age.

The Quilt Revival

By 1900, the merging forces of the Arts and Crafts movement and the Colonial Revival sparked a renewed interest in quilts, which were seriously studied for the first time. Magazine articles appeared, praising their simple designs and honest use of materials.

Two editors played a major role in this Quilt Revival—Gustav Stickley of the *Craftsman* and Edward Bok of the *Ladies' Home Journal.* Both were contemporaries of Marie Webster and both were extremely active in promoting Arts and Crafts ideas to a wider audience.

Gustav Stickley (1858–1942), creator of the austere Craftsman style of furniture, was one of the leaders of the American Arts and Crafts movement. From 1901 to 1916, he published

Gustav Stickley designed this spindle armchair in 1905—a fine example of his durable and handsome Craftsman furniture. (Courtesy of L. & J. G. Stickley, Inc.)

the *Craftsman* magazine, whose motto was "For the simplification of life." He ran articles on William Morris, John Ruskin and the English Arts and Crafts guilds, and featured plans for convenient, reasonably priced houses with comfortable and rustic furnishings.

Stickley advocated unified designs for house interiors. He believed that "silks, plushes and tapestries, in fact delicate and perishable fabrics of all kinds, were utterly out of keeping with Craftsman furniture." Instead he preferred "fabrics that possessed sturdiness and durability, that were made of materials that possessed a certain rugged and straightforward character of fiber, weave and texture—such a character as would bring them into the same class as the sturdy oak and wrought iron and copper of the other furnishings."[2]

One of Stickley's favorite fabrics was hand-loomed linen, decorated with "bold and simple" appliqué designs. "It is," he wrote, "the kind of needlework that any woman can do and, given the power of discrimination and taste in the selection of materials, designs and color combinations, there is no reason why any woman should not, with comparatively little time and labor, make her home interesting with beautiful needlework." In 1907, Stickley even sponsored a competition for appliqué designs. Prizes of Craftsman furniture were awarded for curtains and pillows with flowers, leaves and seed pods appliquéd in linen.[3]

The "bold and simple" patterns of traditional patchwork quilts fit in perfectly with Stickley's views. In August 1908, the *Craftsman* published "Patch Quilts and Philosophy," under the by-line Elizabeth Daingerfield, although the real author was her older sister, Isabella (1864–1944), who was known as "Bessie."[4] In the course of her missionary work in rural Kentucky, Bessie Daingerfield had befriended quiltmakers of the Appalachian Mountains. In this article, she wrote with sensitivity about their isolated lives. "There is much beautiful and skilful handiwork hidden away in these hills," she wrote. "From the cradle to the grave the women make quilts."[5]

Bessie Daingerfield was particularly interested in the designs which had their source in the quiltmaker's firsthand observation of nature. She especially admired a quilt inspired by the mountain lily, "brought out in its own brave colors in the 'patch' and repeated like a ghost flower in the quilting, which made an effect of which no artist need have been ashamed." Bessie continued, "I have always hated the people who called whatever they admired 'a poem,' but that was the word that came to me while this mountain woman told me how her mind had seized and her hands made captive the beauty of the mountain lily in the one form of expression that was her own."[6]

Several of the quilts shown in this *Craftsman* article were later illustrated in the *Ladies' Home Journal*, whose legendary editor, Edward Bok, played a major role in the Quilt Revival. By publishing pictures of traditional quilts and by commissioning original quilt designs, Bok fostered the emerging interest in quilts at the turn of the century.[7] And his encouragement of Marie Webster led to a whole new direction in quilt design.

Born in Holland in 1863, Bok emigrated with his family to Brooklyn, New York, when he was still a small boy. With enormous energy and a flair for publishing, he became the editor of the *Ladies' Home Journal* in 1889 at the age of 26. During his thirty years at the helm, the *Journal* became America's most popular women's magazine, achieving a circulation of some two million before the First World War.

Deeply involved with the Arts and Crafts movement, Bok used his considerable influence to promote its philosophy. As early as the 1890s, the *Ladies' Home Journal* featured houses by innovative architects and designers like Frank Lloyd Wright and Will Bradley. Bok turned many of his projects into full-blown crusades and rallied his readers in campaigns against such social ills as dirty cities, public drinking cups and patent medicines.[8]

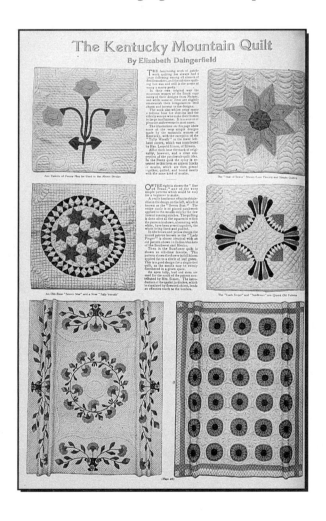

In their own original way the mountain women of the South copy many of their designs from Nature.

– Ladies' Home Journal
Feb. 1912

The Quilt Revival *was promoted by women's magazines of the early 20th century. Bessie Daingerfield's page of Kentucky mountain quilts appeared in the* Ladies' Home Journal *of February 1912. Shown here are Peony (top left), Star of Texas (top right), Seven Star (middle left), Lady Finger, "a quaint old pattern" (middle right), Tulip Wreath (lower left) and Sunflower.*

"Go Straight to Nature"

The needlework section of the *Ladies' Home Journal* also promoted Arts and Crafts ideas. In a 1908 article, "Appliqué Embroidery on Linen," Lilian Wilson suggested a "very fresh and crisp treatment" of hand-woven linen in natural tones, with simple shapes of flowers, leaves and fruit appliquéd onto tablecloths and pillows. "It makes you realize," she said, "how much better it is to go straight to Nature for motifs for decorative art than to keep on wading about in the slough of antiquity." This article could well have inspired Marie Webster's first appliqué quilts.[9]

Edward Bok was a pioneer in the publishing industry. Recognizing the enormous appeal of color to his audience, he published some of the first color covers and advertising to appear in any magazine. These were so successful that, in 1910, he began printing full color illustrations on his fashion and decorating pages.

One day, Bok's needlework editor showed him something sent in by a *Journal* reader—a new quilt with an old-fashioned look, beautifully appliquéd in muted colors. Bok decided to run a full page color feature on quilts. He wrote to the quiltmaker, inviting her to submit more designs. That quiltmaker was Marie Webster and the letter from Bok launched her career as a professional quilt designer.

She had planned the quilt to harmonize with her new Colonial Revival house. Its "Pink Rose" design was her own interpretation of the Rose of Sharon pattern, with a swag border and some new touches, like the pale green lattice which wove the blocks into a unified whole. It was frankly nostalgic—a tribute to the fine hand appliqué work of the past. Her friends and family liked it so much that they persuaded her to send it in to the *Ladies' Home Journal*.

Over the next three years my grandmother contributed 14 designs to the *Journal*. By choosing linen, muslin and solid color cottons, she reflected the Arts and Crafts preference for sturdy materials with a hand-woven look. And for inspiration, she followed Lilian Wilson's suggestion to "go straight to nature" and studied the flowers in her own garden.

Each quilt explored a particular kind of flower, revealing her fascination with the design possiblities of natural forms. Tulips were bent over by the wind, sunflowers crowded together and poppies unfurled their fragile petals. The borders and quilting repeated the main theme, enhancing rather than competing with it. The colors in each quilt were chosen to harmonize with a specific color scheme, in a palette limited to green and several shades of just one other hue—pink, lavender or blue.

The quilting was very important to the overall design. Texture was enhanced by quilting around the outside of each flower and leaf, to give them a three-dimensional quality. Quilted "ghost flowers," like those which were admired by Bessie Daingerfield, echoed the appliqué motifs. Details, such as the veins of leaves or the centers of sunflowers, were shown with quilting stitches. Marie often reserved an area in the center of the quilt for a special quilting design, like the spider webs and blossoms in the Sunflower quilt, or the birds and flowers in Sunbonnet Lassies.

Edward Bok *(1863–1930) was editor of the* Ladies' Home Journal *from 1889 to 1919. (Courtesy of Bok Tower Gardens Archives.)*

Marie used very thin cotton batting, stitched at ¼ to ½ inch intervals—an exacting task. Most of the tops were quilted by other women to her specifications. Residents of the Flinn Home in Marion quilted some of these quilts at a frame set up in one of the parlors, where they gathered to socialize and earn extra money from their needlework skills.[10]

Paintings of four of Marie's quilts—Pink Rose, Iris, Snowflake and Wind-blown Tulip—appeared in the *Ladies' Home Journal's* "New Year's number" of January 1, 1911. These first color pictures of quilts created a sensation among the magazine's readers. Virtually overnight, Marie became a national celebrity—the first quilt designer to gain widespread name recognition.[11]

"The New Patchwork Cushions" of August 1911, showed nine of her pillows with floral motifs—daisies, irises, roses and tulips—appliquéd around a central quilted area.[12]

In January 1912, "The New Flower Patchwork Quilts" featured her most original work.

Instead of using the traditional square block format, these designs broke new ground. Each had a central focus: White Dogwood had blocks set on point with the center block reserved for special quilting, while Morning Glory, Poppy and Sunflower experimented with the medallion style, popular in the early 19th century.[13]

"The Baby's Patchwork Quilt" of August 1912 was the last in the series. "The quilts shown on this page," Marie said, "are practical and sanitary and will give good service…they also may make more welcome the hour of the Sandman's coming." Four were flower quilts: Daisy, Pansies and Butterflies, Morning Glory Wreath and Wild Rose. Her two figurative quilts, Bedtime and Sunbonnet Lassies, were especially charming.[14]

These fourteen Marie Webster quilts from the *Ladies' Home Journal* sparked a revolution in quilt design. They revitalized the art of appliqué with fresh new forms and a palette of pastel colors that would become the hallmark of American quilts in the 1920s and 30s.

A new and artistic note has been achieved in these designs for hand-made quilts of applied patchwork. The aim has been to make them practical as well as beautiful …

– Ladies' Home Journal
Jan. 1911

The Ladies' Home Journal *of January 1, 1911 featured four quilts by Marie Webster—Pink Rose, Snowflake, Iris and Wind-blown Tulip. These first ever color pictures of quilts brought her nationwide fame and launched her career as a professional quilt designer.*

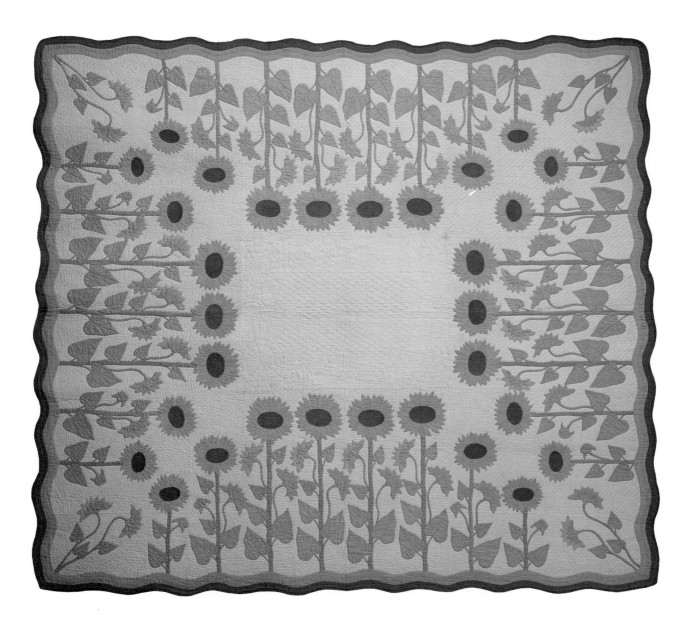

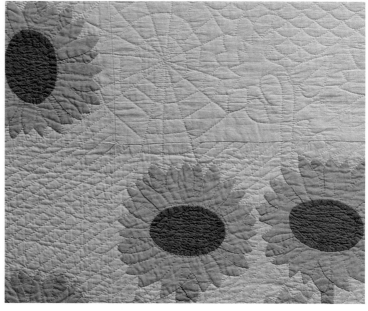

Sunflower. *81" x 89". Linen and cotton. When Marie Webster was designing quilts for the* Ladies' Home Journal, *its editor, Edward Bok, requested that she make a quilt based on the Sunflower, a favorite motif of the Arts and Crafts movement. It must have met with his approval, for he published it in January 1912. Like her Poppy quilt, Marie's Sunflower explores various stages of plant growth. Buds, half-opened flowers and fully mature blossoms rise from a waved border which suggests the earth. The large central area is filled with quilted flowers and spider webs. (©1992 Indianapolis Museum of Art, Webster Collection. Gift of Mrs. Gerrish Thurber.) Pattern begins on p. 80.*

The dogwood quilt offers another good choice in flower designs and one of unusual delicacy and coloring. The full-grown blossoms on the green background remind us delightfully of the beauty of trees and flowers in early spring.

– Ladies' Home Journal
January 1912

White Dogwood. *74" x 91". Linen and cotton. Marie Webster loved the flowers of the dogwood tree, among the earliest to bloom each spring. In this quilt, she set the blocks on point to create a lattice of intersecting branches dotted with pink-tipped blossoms. The background is pale green linen, the branches are of heavily textured linen suggesting bark, while the petals are of smooth white cotton. The focus of the quilt is the wreath of quilted flowers in the center block. Published in the* Ladies' Home Journal *in January 1912, this was her first quilt with a scalloped border, a design feature often used in her later quilts. (Collection of Rosalind Webster Perry.) Pattern begins on page 89.*

*Do not quilt across
any leaves, flowers,
buds or stems,
but around them;
this gives the
raised effect.*

– Marie Webster,
pattern directions

Poppy. *This is a detail of the quilt shown on page 8, made by Marie Webster in 1909. Here, the poppy's life cycle unfolds from bud to delicate blossom to mature seed pod, revealing a fragile and fleeting beauty. Marie's careful observation of nature allowed her to capture the poppies' subtle contours in fabric. Pattern begins on p. 69.*

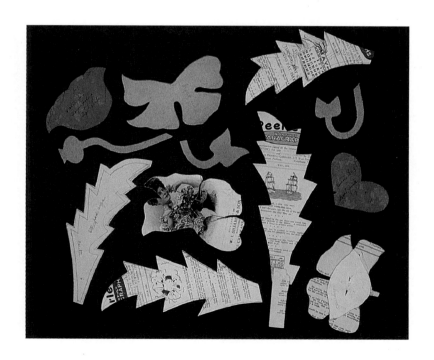

Cardboard Templates *used in cutting out the fabric for Poppy quilt kits made by the Practical Patchwork Company. Poppy continued to be one of Marie Webster's most popular designs in the 1930s, when these templates were being used.*

Sunbonnet Lassies. *38" x 49". Linen, cotton and silk. Designed and made by Marie Webster about 1912. These lassies, with their stylish hats and colorful parasols, are really quite elegant. The quilted background provides a tranquil setting, with a picket fence, nodding sunflowers, and little songbirds flying overhead. Countless appliquéd Sunbonnet Sues and Colonial Ladies may trace their ancestry to this design, first published in the* Ladies' Home Journal *in August 1912. (Collection of Rosalind Webster Perry.) Pattern begins on page 75.*

*The sunbonnet lassies
suggest an outing or
a call from playmates on
the morrow. These lassies
may be dressed in bits of the
gowns of the little maid, and
the quilt thus become a
"keepsake quilt."*

– Ladies' Home Journal
August 1912

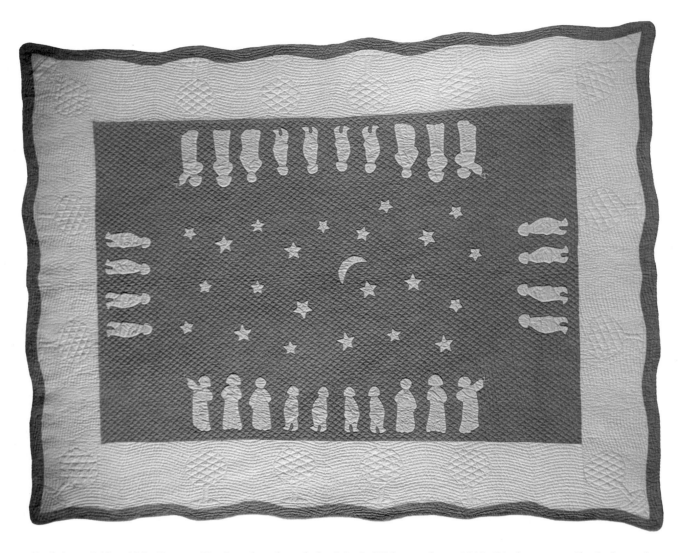

Bedtime. 34" x 45". Cotton. Designed and made by Marie Webster about 1912. Little trees quilted along the white border frame the rows of children dressed in their pajamas and night gowns. It seems they have just stepped into the garden for a moment to admire the crescent moon and starry sky before marching off to bed, candlesticks in hand. (©1992 Indianapolis Museum of Art, Webster Collection. Gift of Mrs. Gerrish Thurber.) Pattern begins on page 41.

The bedtime quilt,
with its procession of
night-clad children, will be
excellent "company" for a tot,
to whom a story may be told of
the things that sleep near the
little trees while the friendly
stars keep watch.

– Ladies' Home Journal
August 1912

*Teach the little
one to tell the petals
of the daisy—
"loves me, loves me not"
—and many happy
moments will be spent
in finding out
whether the child
or his mother
loves the more.*

– Ladies' Home Journal
August 1912

Daisy. *50" x 60". Cotton. Zetta Hanna made this child's quilt in 1991, based on a Webster design in the* Ladies' Home Journal *of August 1912. Quilted daisies are sprinkled along the blue bands. (Collection of Rosalind Webster Perry.) Pattern begins on page 47.*

Zetta Hanna *is a versatile quilter with roots in Indiana, Marie Webster's home state. She now lives in Santa Barbara, California, where she is active in the Coastal Quilters Guild. Zetta especially enjoys fine hand appliqué and quilting.*

Bunnies. 41" x 60". Cotton. Marie Webster designed this pattern about 1914. In 1939, when she was 80 years old, she made the quilt shown here for her little granddaughter. The alternating blocks with white bunnies and Easter baskets are framed by two borders. Brightly colored eggs appliquéd on the inner border appear to be piled in "nests" arrayed along the pink outer border. (Collection of Rosalind Webster Perry.) Pattern begins on page 44.

A full-size tissue paper placement guide for Bunnies was included in Marie Webster's pattern packet.

Grapes and Vines. *76" x 76". Linen and cotton. Marie Webster designed this quilt in 1914, reviving the four-block set which had been popular in the mid-19th century. She added her own innovation—appliquéd sashing strips. The undulating border, similar to the borders of her Sunflower and Bedtime quilts, echoes the long wavy vine on the inner border, adding its own gentle rhythm to the sophisticated design. Nearly 900 appliquéd grapes make this her most challenging pattern. (©1992 Indianapolis Museum of Art, Webster Collection. Gift of Mrs. Gerrish Thurber.) Pattern begins on page 54.*

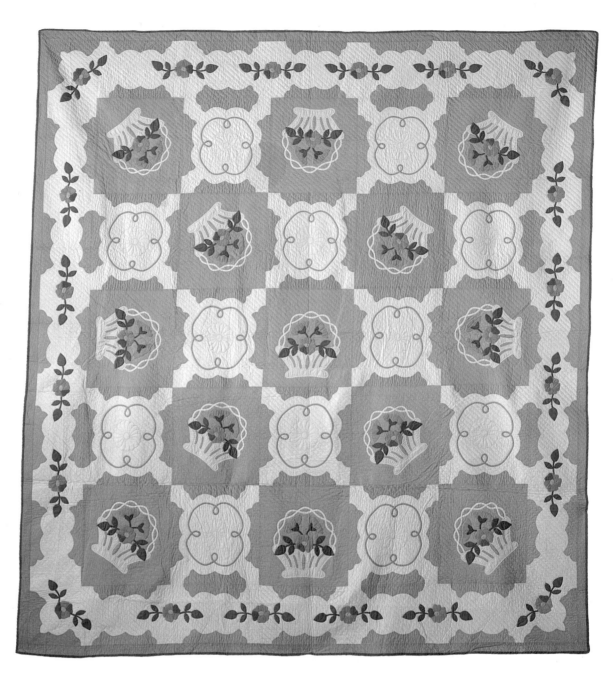

French Baskets. *82" x 92". Cotton. Marie Webster first designed a French Baskets quilt in 1914, with white daisies against a blue background. The quilt shown here, with layered pink roses and a green background, was made about 1930 by Marie's younger sister, Emma Daugherty. The quilt is made up of alternating white and colored blocks, but the green brackets appliquéd onto the white blocks seem to blend with the adjacent green blocks. Reverse appliqué was used to show the background color through the slits in the baskets. (Collection of Katherine Webster Dwight.) Pattern begins on page 50.*

The New Patchwork Quilt Patterns

Demand for the Webster patterns was great. The *Ladies' Home Journal* sold transfer patterns for some of the designs, but Marie had a better idea: she would offer *complete* patterns, including directions, templates and a picture of the finished quilt. Since color selection was very important for the success of each quilt, she also provided fabric swatches, glued to the back of the direction sheet. Another innovation was a full-size placement guide made of colored tissue paper, to show how the appliqué pieces should be layered and arranged.

Her actual directions were extremely brief by today's standards, consisting of only three or four paragraphs, with no diagrams or other visual aids. She advocated the use of washable, colorfast materials. Since these were not always obtainable, she gave instructions for setting "all doubtful shades by soaking in salt water."

The directions continued:

To facilitate the work, starch all linens slightly and iron double, then two designs can be cut at the same time, and the turning under is easier done.... Carefully turn under the edge and baste each piece, clipping the angles and curved edges where necessary. Make stems of narrow bias pieces.

After basting the pieces to the background, the quilter was advised:

Hem all flowers and leaves with corresponding shades of cotton thread. Take out bastings and press on the wrong side. Make the lining the same size as the top, attach to quilting frames, spread the cotton, cover with the top and pin all together smoothly and securely.... Do not quilt across any leaves, flowers, buds or stems, but around them; this gives the raised effect. Any simple design can be used to fill in the space not already covered. Bind the edge with a narrow strip of linen.

Marie's family soon became involved in her burgeoning pattern business. Her sister, Emma Daugherty, took on the task of assembling the tissue paper guides, while her son, an engineer, made blueprints of the patterns—a cheap and accurate method of reproduction. He also drafted the masters for these blueprints, which became a trademark of her patterns. In 1911, "Marie D. Webster's New Quilt Patterns" sold for 50 cents a piece—a price that never varied during the entire 30-year life of her business.

Between 1912 and 1920, she created ten more original designs: Bunnies, Grapes and Vines, French Baskets, Daffodils and Butterflies, Wreath of Roses, Magpie Rose, Poinsettia, Clematis in Bloom, Nasturtium Wreath and Cherokee Rose.[15] Her ideas were continually evolving. In Poinsettia, she experimented with bright colors, a challenging set and patterned fabrics, while in Grapes and Vines she used a four-block set. Wreath of Roses and French Baskets—both published in the *Ladies' Home Journal*—were among her most popular designs.

Tissue paper guide
for Sunbonnet Lassies.
The quilting design—
a picket fence—was
drawn in pencil
on the background.

Poinsettia. 63" x 94 ½". Cotton and linen. A trip to California inspired Marie Webster to make this vibrant quilt, finished in 1917. By setting the blocks on point and using a striking black and white striped fabric for the sashing and borders, she captured the excitement of these gorgeous winter blooms. (© 1992 Indianapolis Museum of Art, Webster Collection. Gift of Mrs. Gerrish Thurber.) Pattern begins on page 65.

Poinsettia details (below). Marie chose a yellow print fabric for the flower centers—one of the few times she did not use a solid color. In a subtle touch, the largest petals on the half blocks slightly overlap the borders.

May Tulips. *76" x 87 ½". Cotton. This twin bed quilt was one of a pair made about 1933 by Marie Webster's sister, Emma Daugherty, who also made the French Baskets quilt on page 29. Marie designed the pattern in the early 1920s and it became one of her most popular. (Private collection.) Pattern begins on page 62.*

Stamped and basted block. *This is a partially completed block from a May Tulips kit. Each numbered piece was prepared by basting the turn-under allowances before it was basted onto the muslin block. The May 1931 issue of* Needlecraft *magazine advertised stamped blocks in the May Tulips pattern for 25 cents each. A complete kit for a double bed quilt cost only $3.65!*

America's First Quilt Book

Marie Webster was very quickly recognized as the nation's leading quiltmaker. In 1912, Doubleday, Page & Company, the New York publisher, asked her to write a history of quilts. Because of her lifelong interest in both needlework and history, my grandmother accepted the challenge and became an author.

Quilts: Their Story and How to Make Them was published in 1915 and has become a classic. In a lively style much quoted by later writers, she traced the origins of appliqué and quilting back to the Renaissance, the Middle Ages and even to ancient Egypt. She stressed the importance of quilts in the American experience and included examples of pioneer folklore as well as humorous anecdotes. Her thorough research, including a list of over 400 pattern names, has made the book a valuable reference work.

Marie believed that quiltmaking should be recognized as an art form. Urging appreciation of the anonymous women artists who created beauty with their needles, she wrote: *The work of the old-time quilters possesses artistic merit to a very high degree. While much of it was designed strictly for utilitarian purposes—in fact, more for rugged service than display, yet the number of beautiful old quilts which these industrious ancestors have bequeathed to us is very large. Every now and then there comes to light one of these old quilts of the most exquisite loveliness, in which the needlework is almost painful in its exactness. Such treasures are worthy of study and imitation, and are deserving of careful preservation for the inspiration of future generations of quilters.*[16]

My grandmother collected dozens of photographs of heirloom quilts to illustrate her book. Most were appliqué quilts, reflecting her own preference for the style. These pictures have inspired many other fine quilters to create their own masterpieces, like the Indiana Wreath quilts made by Rose Kretsinger and Charlotte Jane Whitehill, based on the book's frontispiece.[17]

Quilts: Their Story and How to Make Them was acclaimed by its readers and was reviewed by more than twenty publications, including the *New York Times*, the *Christian Science Monitor*, the *Chicago Tribune* and *Craftsman* magazine. The author received an avalanche of mail from as far away as England, Finland, Hawaii, China, India and New Zealand. Prominent collectors, antique dealers, decorators and social reformers wrote to her, as did thousands of ordinary women who were delighted with this account of their favorite pastime.[18]

Marie was invited to speak to many groups, as varied as the Mississippi Centennial Exposition, the Wabash Literary Circle and the Indianapolis Women's Prison. She gave a truly memorable lecture, attired in an old-fashioned green silk gown with a wide lace collar and flowing bell sleeves, and her hair done in ringlets. She displayed some of her own designs as well as quilts she had collected. On occasion, her friends—also dressed in Early American costumes—would accompany her. After the lecture was over, they would entertain the guests by giving quilting demonstrations and singing quilting songs!

She continued to promote quilting in many ways, until her retirement at the age of 80. She often judged the quilt contests that proliferated during the 1920s and 30s, and sometimes offered a prize for the best original design. This involvement of "America's best known quilt expert" encouraged pride in fine workmanship among a wide audience.[19]

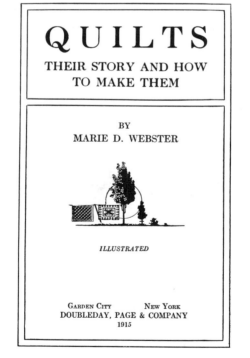

QUILTS

THEIR STORY AND HOW TO MAKE THEM

BY
MARIE D. WEBSTER

ILLUSTRATED

GARDEN CITY　　NEW YORK
DOUBLEDAY, PAGE & COMPANY
1915

Marie Webster and friends, Marion, Indiana, about 1905. Marie is seated in the middle row, second from left.

The Webster's garden made a pleasant setting for summer gatherings. Marie served refreshments to her husband George (left) and two friends, about 1915.

Marie Webster with her grandchildren, Katherine Marie (left) and Rosalind.

Marie Webster and friends in the 1920s. Marie is second from the left.

The Practical Patchwork Company

After World War I, Marie's pattern business expanded and flourished. In 1921, two close friends, Ida Hess and Evangeline Beshore, joined her in starting the Practical Patchwork Company to market both kits and finished quilts in the popular Webster patterns.

Their motto was the famous phrase "A Thing of Beauty is a Joy Forever," from a poem by John Keats. They advertised in women's magazines and issued a series of catalogs called "Quilts and Spreads." Prices ranged from $65 to $100 for a full-size finished quilt, $35 for a basted quilt and only $5 for a baby quilt kit.

The Practical Patchwork Company always remained a cottage industry, with Marie's family continuing to help. Her sister, Emma, made the tissue paper guides, her son drew the blueprints during his holiday visits, and her husband answered correspondance when Marie was traveling.

The partners did all the basting and appliqué themselves, but the quilting was usually done by others. Many of these expert quilters were members of church groups who quilted together for the benefit of their parish, charging $20 to $30 per quilt. One such group was the Rebecca Herd Missionary Society of the Presbyterian Church in Booneville, Kentucky, which numbered up to 18 members, sitting around two quilting frames. They gathered monthly from the 1920s until 1990, when only two members were still active.[20]

During the 1920s, the style of Marie's quilts changed. She simplified the outlines of the flowers and eliminated difficult curves and sharp angles. Since colorfast cottons in bright pastels had become available, she used a more varied palette in many of her quilts. Art Deco's streamlined forms and geometric motifs were becoming fashionable. Marie's multicolored May Tulips and Rainbow quilts, with geometric borders and simpler shapes, are typical of her later style.

Practical Patchwork continued to thrive until the outbreak of World War II. It sold kits and patterns all across the country and even overseas, by mail order, through department stores like Chicago's Marshall Field as well as in specialty outlets like Mary McElwain's famous quilt shop in Wisconsin. Other pattern companies also marketed these designs, often changing the names so they were no longer recognized as Webster patterns. To give just two examples, Mrs. Danner's Quilts called French Baskets "Ivory Baskets," while May Tulips was sold as "Trailing Tulips."[21]

Today, we are experiencing a renaissance in the art of appliqué, which has revived interest in Marie Webster's quilts. Pages could be filled with the names of books and magazines which have published her designs.[22] These patterns, so influential in the early decades of this century, are once again inspiring new generations of quiltmakers. In fact, the impact of her work has been felt far beyond anything Marie could have imagined when, at the age of fifty, she created her first appliqué quilt.

Quilters, remember, as you stitch your favorite pattern, that you are in good company—the thousands of quilt lovers who, over the years, have truly discovered "a joy forever" in Marie Webster's designs!

A tablecloth design sold by the *Practical Patchwork Company.*

Notes

1 See also "Marie Webster: Her Story" by Rosalind Webster Perry in *Quilts: Their Story and How to Make Them* by Marie D. Webster, (Santa Barbara: Practical Patchwork, 1990), pp. 204–224.

2 Gustav Stickley, *Craftsman Homes: Architecture and Furnishings of the American Arts and Crafts Movement* (1909; New York: Dover Publications, 1979), pp. 165–166.

3 Stickley, *Craftsman Homes,* p. 168 and "Prize Winners of the Craftsman Competition in Designs for Textile Decoration in Appliqué," *Craftsman,* vol. 13, no. 5 (Feb. 1908), pp. 599–604.

4 Personal communication from Keene Daingerfield, 15 June 1991.

5 Elizabeth Daingerfield, "Patch Quilts and Philosophy," *Craftsman,* vol. 14 (August 1908), pp. 523–527.

6 Daingerfield, p. 525.

7 The two articles in the *Ladies' Home Journal* with Elizabeth Daingerfield's byline were: "Kentucky Mountain Patchwork Quilts" (July 1909) and "The Kentucky Mountain Quilt" (Feb. 1912). Other quilt features in the *Journal* during Bok's tenure include: Sybil Lanigan, "Revival of the Patchwork Quilt" (Oct. 1894); Jane Benson, "Designs for Patchwork Quilt" (Nov. 1896); a series of original appliqué designs by well known artists: Ernest Thompson Seton, "A Wild-Animal Bedquilt" (Jan. 1905), Maxfield Parrish, "A Circus Bedquilt" (March 1905), Gazo Foudji, "A Dragon Bedquilt" (May 1905), Peter Newell, "An Alice in Wonderland Bedquilt" (Sept. 1905), Jessie Willcox Smith, "A Child's Good-Night Bedquilt" (Nov. 1905); also Lilian Barton Wilson, "Appliqué Embroidery on Linen" (Jan. 1908); and Mrs. Leopold Simon, "When Patchwork Becomes an Art" (Aug. 1908).

8 Edward Bok's Pulitzer Prize-winning autobiography, *The Americanization of Edward Bok* (New York: Scribner's, 1920), pp. 244–245.

9 Lilian Barton Wilson, "Appliqué Embroidery on Linen," *Ladies' Home Journal* (Jan. 1908), p. 41.

10 A photograph of two women quilting at the Flinn Home appears in Marie Webster's *Quilts: Their Story and How to Make Them.* (Fig. 65 in the 1990 edition.)

11 *Ladies' Home Journal* (1 Jan. 1911), p. 25. A pattern for Pink Rose (called "Rose of Sharon") is in *Quilts Galore!* by Diana McClun and Laura Nownes (San Francisco: Quilt Digest Press, 1990), pp. 100–102. A pattern for Wind-blown Tulips is available from Stearns Technical Textiles Co. (Mountain Mist) and can also be found in *50 Country Quilting Projects,* edited by Margit Echols (Emmaus, PA: Rodale Press, 1990), pp. 171–178.

12 *Ladies' Home Journal* (August 1911), p. 25.

13 *Ladies' Home Journal* (January 1912), p. 38.

14 *Ladies' Home Journal* (August 1912), p. 27.

15 Three of these were published: Wreath of Roses in the *Ladies' Home Journal* (Oct. 1915), p. 43; French Baskets in the *Ladies' Home Journal* (Feb. 1918), p. 110; and Cherokee Rose in *Needlecraft,* (Sept. 1930), p. 25.

16 Webster, *Quilts: Their Story and How to Make Them.* (1990), pp. xxiii–xxiv.

17 Rose Kretsinger's Indiana Wreath, made in 1927, is in the Spencer Museum of Art. Charlotte Jane Whitehill's quilt, now in the Denver Art Museum, was made in 1930. Both quilts have been exhibited in Japan; see *American Patchwork Quilt* (The Denver Art Museum, 1986), Fig. 1, and *American Patchwork Quilt* (Spencer Museum of Art, University of Kansas, 1987), Plate 42.

18 A number of these letters are quoted in the biography of Marie Webster in the 1990 edition of *Quilts: Their Story and How to Make Them,* pp. 213–216.

19 See the Indiana Quilt Project's *Quilts of Indiana* (Bloomington: Indiana University Press, 1991), pp. 120–121, for a prize-winning quilt judged by Marie Webster and her colleagues Evangeline Beshore and Ida (Hess) Lillard in 1930.

20 Interviews with Cora Baker and Ann Eversole, June 1991.

21 Cuesta Benberry, "Marie D. Webster: A Major Influence on Quilt Design in the 20th Century," *Quilter's Newsletter Magazine,* no. 224 (July/August 1990), p. 32; and "Marie Webster: Indiana's Gift to American Quilts" in *Quilts of Indiana,* pp. 88–93.

22 A partial list appears in the 1990 edition of *Quilts: Their Story and How to Make Them,* p. 224.

Bibliography

An American Sampler: Folk Art from the Shelburne Museum. Washington, DC: National Gallery of Art, 1987.

Anscombe, Isabelle and Charlotte Gere. *Arts & Crafts in Britain and America.* New York: Rizzoli, 1978.

Axelrod, Alan, ed. *The Colonial Revival in America.* New York: W.W. Norton for Henry Francis du Pont Winterthur Museum, 1985.

Benberry, Cuesta. "Stearns and Foster–Part III." *Quilters' Journal*, vol. 4, no. 2 (1981), pp. 13-15.

——. "The 20th Century's First Quilt Revival." *Quilter's Newsletter*, no. 114 (July/Aug. 1979), pp. 20-22; no. 115 (Sept. 1979), pp. 25-29; no. 116 (Oct. 1979), pp. 10-11.

——. "Marie D. Webster: A Major Influence on Quilt Design in the 20th Century." *Quilter's Newsletter Magazine*, no. 224 (July/Aug. 1990), pp. 32-35.

——. "Marie Webster: Indiana's Gift to American Quilts." In *Quilts of Indiana.* Indiana Quilt Registry Project. Bloomington: Indiana University Press, 1991.

Bok, Edward W. *The Americanization of Edward Bok.* New York: Charles Scribner's Sons, 1921.

——. *Twice Thirty.* New York: Charles Scribner's, 1925.

Callen, Anthea. *Angel in the Studio: Women in the Arts and Crafts Movement 1870-1914.* London: Astragal Books, 1979.

Clark, Robert Judson, ed. *The Arts and Crafts Movement in America 1876-1916.* Princeton, NJ: Princeton University Press, 1972.

Daingerfield, Elizabeth. "Patch Quilts and Philosophy." *The Craftsman*, Aug. 1908, pp. 523-527.

———. "Kentucky Mountain Patchwork Quilts." *Ladies' Home Journal*, July 1909.

——. "The Kentucky Mountain Quilt." *Ladies' Home Journal*, Feb. 1912.

Gunn, Virginia. "Quilts for Milady's Boudoir." In *Uncoverings 1989*, edited by Laurel Horton. San Francisco: American Quilt Study Group, 1990.

Handlin, David P. *The American Home: Architecture and Society, 1815–1915.* Boston: Little, Brown, 1979.

Lasansky, Jeannette. *Pieced by Mother: Over 100 Years of Quiltmaking Traditions.* Lewisburg, PA: Oral Traditions Project of the Union Co. Historical Society, 1987.

McElwain, Mary A. *The Romance of Village Quilts.* Walworth, WI: 1936.

McMorris, Penny. *Crazy Quilts.* New York: E.P. Dutton, 1984.

Naylor, Gillian. *The Arts and Crafts Movement.* (1971) Reprint. London: Trefoil Publications, 1990.

Paydar, Niloo Imami. *Marie Webster Quilts: A Retrospective.* Indianapolis: Indianapolis Museum of Art, 1991.

Perry, Rosalind Webster. "Marie Webster: Marion's Master Quilter." *Traces of Indiana and Midwestern History*, vol. 3, no. 2 (Spring 1991), pp. 28–31.

Steinberg, Salme Harju. *Reformer in the Marketplace: Edward W. Bok and The Ladies' Home Journal.* Baton Rouge, LA: Louisiana State University Press, 1979.

Waldvogel, Merikay. *Soft Covers for Hard Times: Quiltmaking & the Great Depression.* Nashville, TN: Rutledge Hill Press, 1990.

Watkinson, Ray. *William Morris as Designer.* London: Trefoil Publications, 1990.

Webster, Marie D. *Quilts: Their Story and How to Make Them.* New York: Doubleday, Page, 1915. Reprint with additional material by Rosalind Webster Perry. Santa Barbara, CA: Practical Patchwork, 1990.

——. "The New Patchwork Quilt." *Ladies' Home Journal*, 1 Jan. 1911, p. 25.

——. "The New Patchwork Cushions." *Ladies' Home Journal*, Aug. 1911, p. 25.

——. "The New Flower Patchwork Quilts." *Ladies' Home Journal*, Jan. 1912, p. 38.

——. "The Baby's Patchwork Quilt." *Ladies' Home Journal*, Aug. 1912, p. 27.

——. "A Rose Patchwork Bedroom." *Ladies' Home Journal*, Oct. 1915, p. 43.

——. "The Coverlet and Cushion." *Ladies' Home Journal*, Feb. 1918, p. 110.

——. "Pink Dogwood in Appliqué for the Bedroom." *Ladies' Home Journal*, Sept. 1927, p. 92.

——. "The Cherokee Rose Quilt." *Needlecraft*, Sept. 1930, p. 25. Reprinted in *Quilter's Newsletter Magazine*, May 1985, p. 42.

——. "The May Tulip in Applique." *Needlecraft*, May 1931, p. 6.

Woodard, Thos. K. & Blanche Greenstein. *Twentieth Century Quilts 1900-1950.* New York: E.P. Dutton, 1988.

ASSEMBLY

- Use a ¼" seam allowance when assembling the quilt top.

- When blocks are set straight, as in Bunnies or French Baskets, sew together rows of blocks and then sew the rows together to complete the quilt top.

- When blocks are set on point, as in Poinsettia or White Dogwood, sew the diagonal rows together and then sew the rows together.

BORDERS

- The quilts in this book have several different types of borders. Some quilts, such as Sunbonnet Lassies and Iris, have multiple straight borders. First piece together the border strips into units and then sew the units to the partially assembled quilt top.

- Several quilts have appliquéd waved borders. Using the border guides provided, mark the borders and cut on the lengthwise grain. Also mark placement of the borders on the quilt top. Appliqué only the inner edge of the waved borders before basting and quilting. To prepare the quilt for binding, trim all layers ¼" from marked line of outer edge of waved borders.

- May Tulips has a scalloped border. To prepare the quilt for binding, use the border template and mark the sewing line along the outer edge of the border. Trim ¼" outside of the marked line, then bind.

- Most of these quilts have either mitered or squared border corners, but some, like Bedtime and Iris, have both. Instructions for sewing border corners can be found in any basic quiltmaking book. See our Suggested Reading section for some recommended titles.

BATTING

- Marie Webster always used a very thin cotton batting, for a lightweight and elegant quilt. Today, you can achieve the same effect by choosing either 100% cotton, cotton/polyester or light polyester batting.

QUILTING

- The quilting on these quilts is both extensive and beautiful. In most cases, Marie hired other women to do the quilting to her specifications. She often used variations of her appliqué designs for quilting templates, as in Daisy and Poppy. Close quilting was necessary to secure the cotton batting, with quilting lines sometimes only ¼" or even ⅛" apart. Simple background designs were preferred, like those shown below.

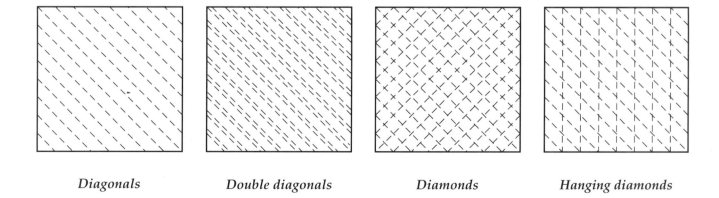

Diagonals   *Double diagonals*   *Diamonds*   *Hanging diamonds*

Bedtime

FINISHED SIZES

Quilt: 34" x 45"
Center rectangle: 23" x 34"
Inner border: 4½" wide
Outer border: 1" wide
Binding: ¼" wide

YARDAGE

1½ yards white for children, stars, moon and
   inner border
1½ yards blue for center rectangle and outer
   border
1½ yards for backing
½ yard blue for binding

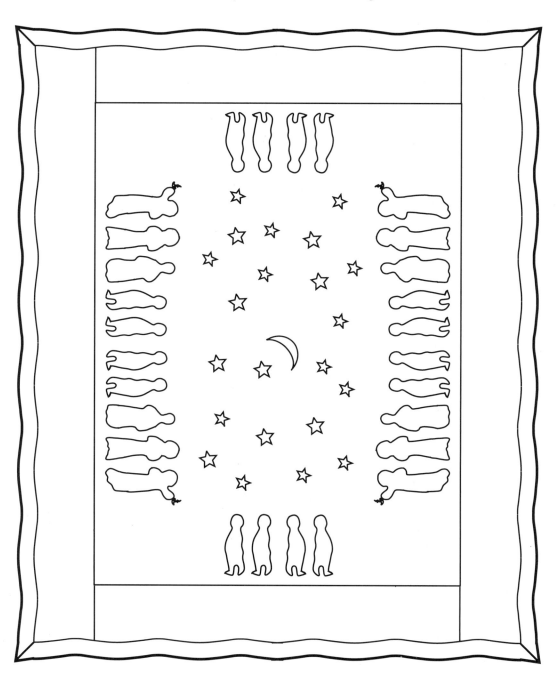

CUTTING

White
2 inner borders 6¼" x 23½"
2 inner borders 6¼" x 45½"
2 A children
2 A reversed children
2 B children
2 B reversed children
2 C children
2 C reversed children
8 D children
8 D reversed children
1 E moon
9 F large stars
13 G small stars

Blue
Center rectangle 23½ " x 34½"
2 outer borders 1¾" x 34½"
2 outer borders 1¾" x 45½"

Binding
Cut bias strips 1¼" wide for
¼" finished single fold binding.

ASSEMBLY

1. Complete appliqué on the center rectangle. The children are arranged so that they face towards the corners. Place 2 D and 2 D reversed children along the center of each side. On the long sides, add one C, B and A child to either end of the row of D children. Appliqué the moon and scatter the stars in the center of the rectangle. With white thread, embroider candlesticks and flames.

2. Sew short white inner borders to short sides of the center rectangle. Add long inner borders to long sides.

3. Using the guide provided, mark the waved pattern on the blue outer borders. Also mark placement of waved borders on white inner borders. The wave repeats approximately 7 times along the long side and 6 times along the short side. Appliqué inner edge of blue borders over white inner borders, with the outer raw edges even. Miter the corners. Baste outer edge of waved borders to quilt top.

4. Layer quilt top, batting and backing, then baste.

5. Quilt around outside of all appliquéd pieces. Quilt details on children's clothing. Quilt blue rectangle with diamonds. Quilt tree designs in corners and along white inner borders. Fill background of white border with waved lines that echo the curves of the waved border.

6. Trim all layers ¼" from marked outer edge of waved border. Bind with blue.

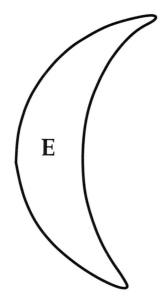

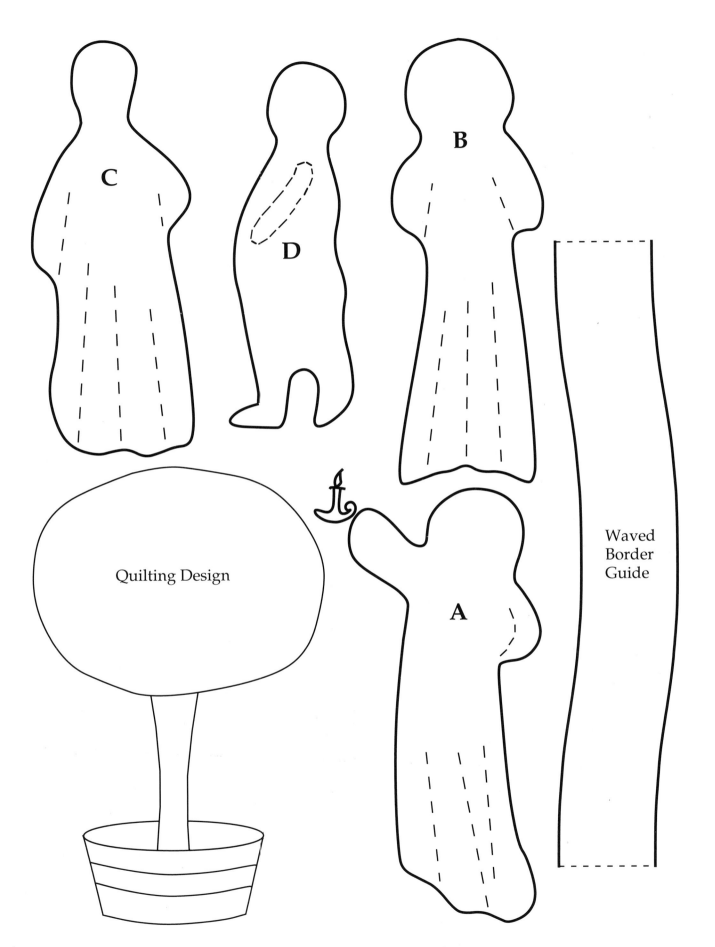

C

D

B

A

Quilting Design

Waved
Border
Guide

Bunnies

FINISHED SIZES

Quilt: 40" x 58"
Blocks: 9" x 9"
Inner borders: 3" at the widest
Outer border:s 3½" at the widest
Binding: ¼" wide

YARDAGE

2 yards white for blocks, bunnies and inner borders
1¾ yards pink for blocks, baskets and outer border
Scraps of different colors for eggs
1¾ yards for backing
½ yard dark pink for binding

Cutting

White
2 inner borders 3½" x 27½"
2 inner borders 3½" x 51½"
7 blocks 9½" x 9½"
4 A bunnies
4 A reversed bunnies
12 B bunnies
12 B reversed bunnies
10 C bunnies
10 C reversed bunnies

Pink
2 outer borders 4" x 33½"
2 outer borders 4" x 58½"
8 blocks 9½" x 9½"
7 D baskets

Scraps
Cut 140 E eggs from various colors.

Binding
Cut bias strips 1¼" wide for ¼" finished single fold binding.

Quilting Design

Assembly

1. Complete appliqué on 15 blocks. Appliqué 1 A, 1 B and 1 C bunny on each pink block, referring to picture of quilt for placement of bunnies and reversed bunnies. Mark position of D basket on each white block. Appliqué a few eggs that will be partly concealed by the basket. Then appliqué 1 D basket onto each white block, overlapping the eggs. Add more eggs until there are 8 in each basket, varying the colors.

2. Join the appliquéd blocks, alternating pink and white blocks as shown.

3. Sew short white borders and then long white borders to the assembled blocks.

4. Using nest guides provided, mark large and small nests on the pink borders. Also mark placement of nests on white borders. The short borders have 1 large nest and 2 small nests. The long borders have 1 large nest and 4 small nests. Appliqué pink borders onto white borders.

5. Appliqué eggs onto the white inner borders, varying the colors. Each short border has one group of 6 eggs in the middle and 2 groups of 3 eggs. Each long border has one group of 6 eggs in the middle and 4 groups of 3 eggs. Each corner has one group of 6 eggs.

6. Appliqué bunnies onto pink outer borders, referring to picture of quilt for placement of bunnies and reversed bunnies. Each short border has 3 B bunnies and 2 C bunnies. Each long border has 5 B bunnies and 4 C bunnies.

7. Layer quilt top, batting and backing, then baste.

8. Quilt around the appliquéd pieces. Quilt basket with diamonds. If you wish, use bunny quilting design next to baskets. Complete quilting with diagonals or other simple background design.

9. Bind with dark pink.

Cutting

Blue
5 bands 6" x 60"

White
4 bands 6" x 60"
5 A petals
5 A reversed petals
5 B petals
5 B reversed petals
14 D half-daisies
14 D reversed half-daisies

Green
From ¾ yard, cut ¾" wide bias
   strips for stems.
From ¼ yard, cut
   10 E leaves
   10 E reversed leaves

Yellow
10 C centers

Backing
Cut the 4 yards into two 2-yard
pieces. From one piece, cut two
strips 8" x 2 yards. Sew these
strips lengthwise to either side
of the other 2-yard piece.

Binding
Cut bias strips 1¼" wide for ¼"
finished single fold binding.

Assembly

1. Sew the bands together lengthwise, alternating blue and white bands.

2. Appliqué stems first, then E leaves and D half-daisies. For full daisies, appliqué A petals and overlap with B petals, referring to Placement Diagram. Appliqué C centers to cover the sharp angles on A and B petals.

3. Layer quilt top, batting and backing, then baste.

4. Quilt around all appliqué pieces. Quilt veins on the leaves. Using quilting template, quilt daisies along the blue bands. Quilt the background with diagonals or any other simple design.

5. Bind with blue.

Quilting Design

A

E

B

C

D

Placement Diagram

Quilting Design

E

F

G

A

fold

Placement Diagram

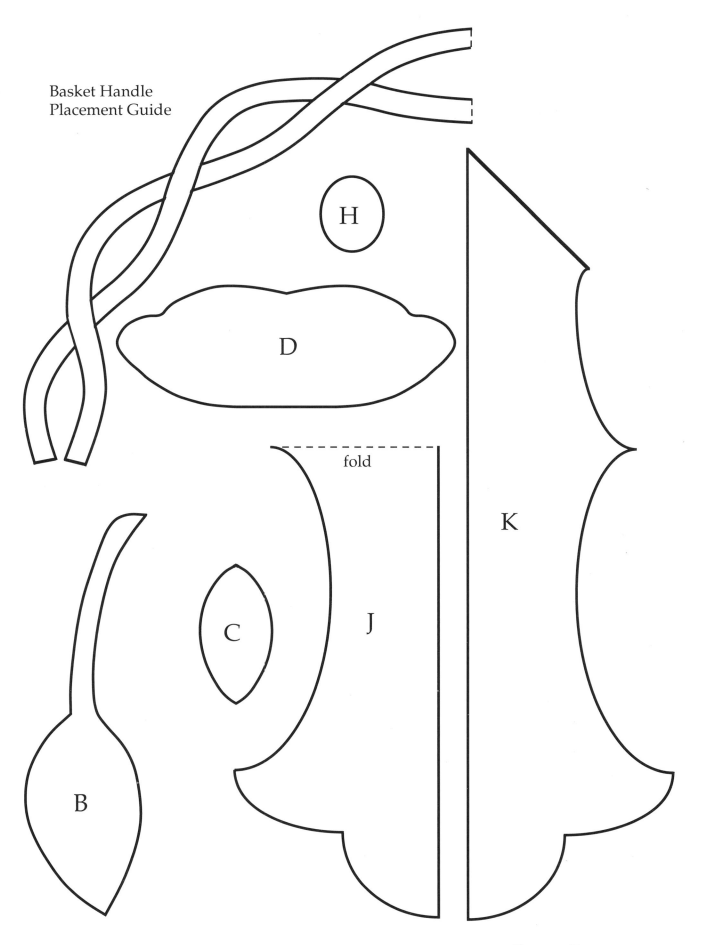

Basket Handle
Placement Guide

H

D

fold

J

K

C

B

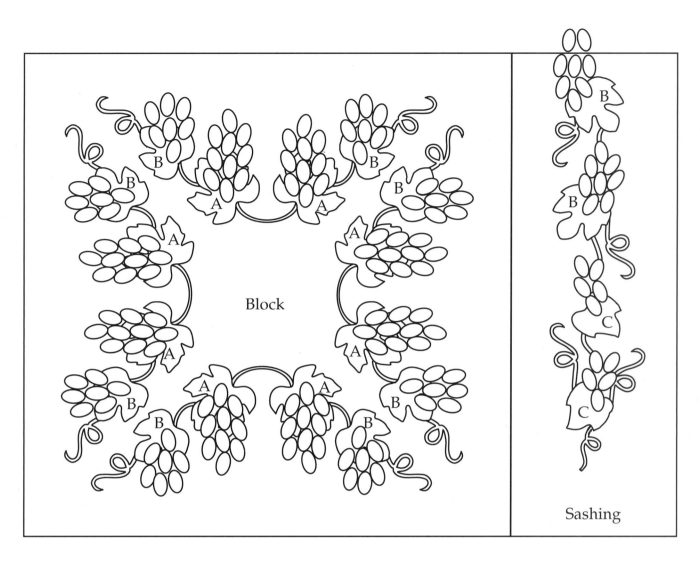

Block

Sashing

Diagram 1

Border

Diagram 2

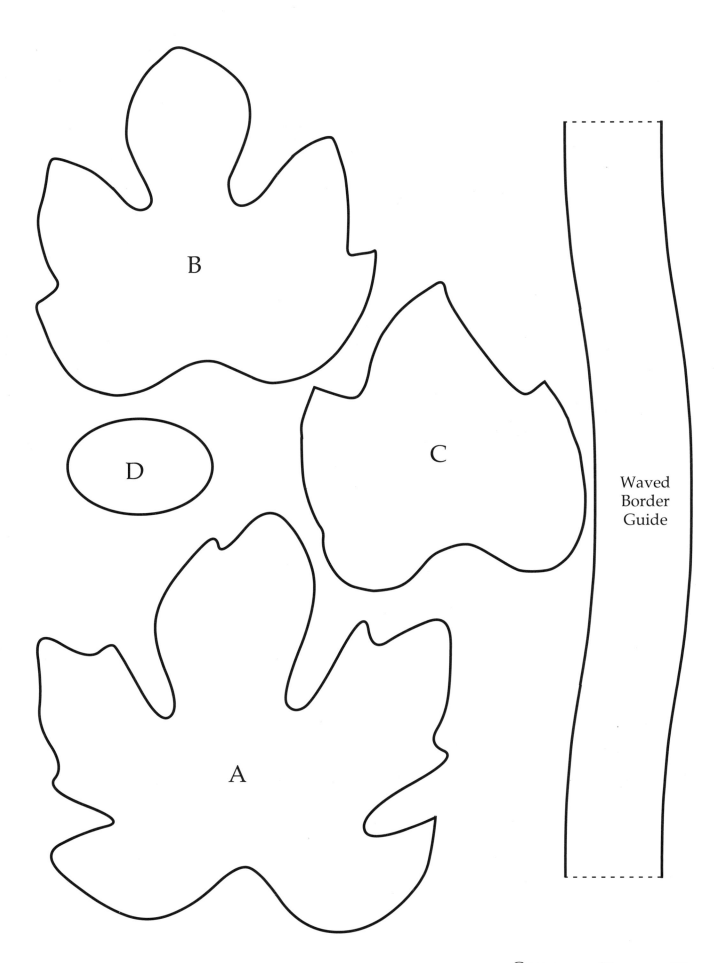

Waved
Border
Guide

Iris

Finished Sizes

Quilt: 83½" x 83½"
Blocks: 21½" x 21½"
Inner borders: 6½" wide
Outer borders: each 1" wide
Binding: ¼" wide

Yardage

6 yards white for blocks and borders
2½ yards dark lavender for petals and border
2½ yards medium lavender for flowers, buds
 and border
1 yard light lavender for flowers, petals and buds
3¾ yards green for stems and leaves
5 yards for backing
¾ yard dark lavender for binding

CUTTING

White
Cut 6 yards of fabric into 2 pieces, one 2½ yards long and one 3½ yards long.
From the 2½-yard piece, cut
    2 inner borders 7" x 78"
    2 inner borders 7" x 65"
    4 outer borders 1½" x 84"
From the 3½-yard piece, cut
    9 blocks 22" x 22".

Dark Lavender
4 outer borders 1½" x 84"
28 C petals for borders

Medium Lavender
4 outer borders 1½" x 84"
72 A flowers for blocks
40 D buds
40 D reversed buds

Light Lavender
28 B flowers for borders
72 C petals for blocks
36 D buds for blocks
36 D reversed buds for blocks

Green
From ¾ yard, cut ¾" wide bias for stems.
Cut bias into strips as follows:
    36 strips 7"long for blocks
    36 strips 3½" long for blocks
    24 strips 1½" long for borders
    4 strips 4½" long for corners
From 3 yards, cut
    76 E bud stems
    76 E reversed bud stems
    72 F leaves for blocks
    72 F reversed leaves for blocks
    24 G leaves for borders
    24 G reversed leaves for borders
    4 H leaves for corners
    4 H reversed leaves for corners

Backing
Cut 5 yards into two 2½-yard pieces.
Seam lengthwise.

Binding
Cut bias strips 1¼" wide for ¼" finished single fold binding.

ASSEMBLY

1. Complete appliqué on 9 blocks, referring to Diagram 1 for placement. For each block, appliqué four 7½" and four 3½" stems, 8 medium lavender A flowers, 8 light lavender C petals, 8 light and 8 medium D buds, 16 E bud stems and 16 F leaves. The raw edge of the base of the F leaves will be caught in the block seams.

2. Assemble the 9 blocks. The bases of the leaves in adjacent blocks should touch each other.

3. Complete appliqué on inner borders, referring to Diagram 2. Each border iris consists of 1 light lavender B flower, 1 dark lavender C petal, one 1½" stem and 2 G leaves. Each corner iris consists of 1 light lavender B flower, 1 dark lavender C petal, one 4½" stem, 2 medium lavender D buds, 2 E bud stems and 2 H leaves. Appliqué 6 border irises on the short borders, and 6 border irises and 2 corner irises on the long borders.

4. Sew the 2 short appliquéd borders to the partially assembled quilt top, then add the 2 long appliquéd borders.

5. For each outer border unit, sew together a medium lavender strip, a white strip and a dark lavender strip, in that order. With the dark lavender on the outside, sew the outer border units to the quilt top. Miter the corner seams.

6. Layer quilt top, batting and backing, then baste.

7. Quilt around all appliquéd flowers, buds, stems and leaves. You may use the B flower as a quilting template to quilt iris designs in the center of each block and on the border. Finish quilting with diagonals or any other simple design.

8. Bind with dark lavender.

Diagram 1: Block Placement

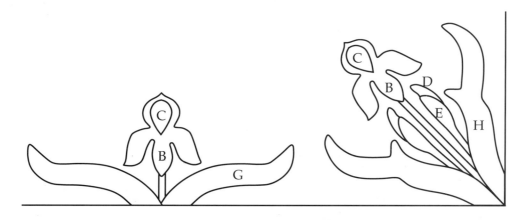

Diagram 2: Border Placement

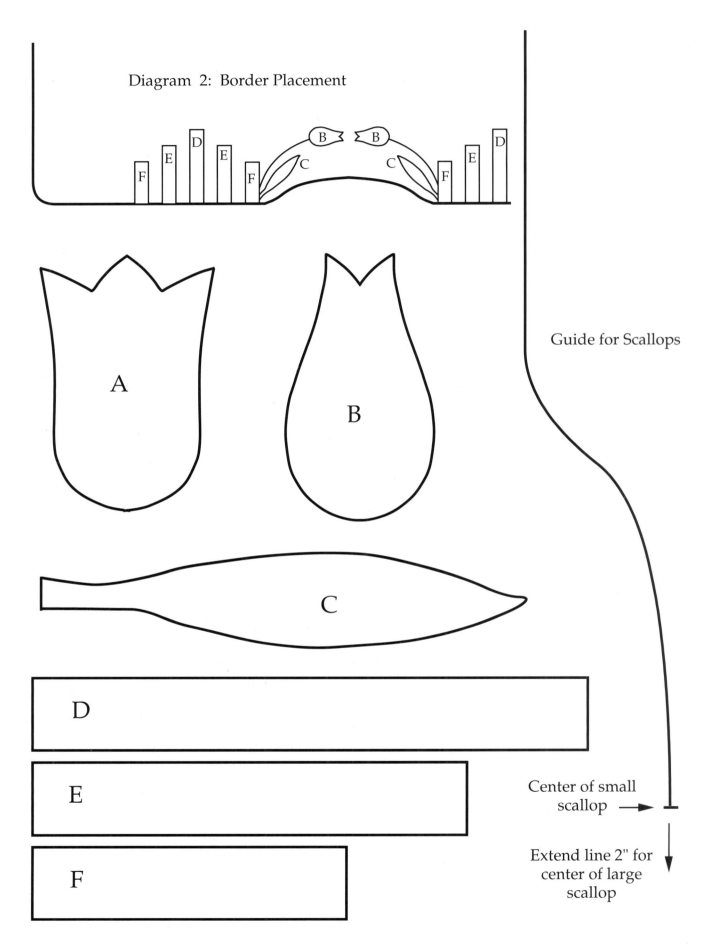

Diagram 2: Border Placement

Guide for Scallops

A

B

C

D

E

F

Center of small scallop →

Extend line 2" for center of large scallop

Poinsettia

FINISHED SIZES

Quilt: 63" x 94½"
Blocks: 10" x 10"
Sashing: 1¼" wide
Wide inner borders: 6½" wide
Narrow outer borders: 1" wide
Binding: ¼" wide

YARDAGE

3 yards white for blocks and triangles
4 yards stripes for sashing and inner borders
    Note: Fabric shown has cross-grain stripes.
¾ yard green for leaves
¼ yard yellow for flower centers
3 yards red for petals and outer borders
6 yards for backing
¾ yard red for binding

CUTTING

White
23 blocks 10½" x 10½"

Cut 3 squares 15½" x 15½". Cut each square into quarters diagonally to make a total of 12 large triangles. (See Diagram 1.)

Cut 2 squares 8" x 8". Cut each square in half diagonally to make a total of 4 small triangles. (See Diagram 2.)

Stripes
2 inner borders 7" x 63½"
2 inner borders 7" x 95"

Cut remaining fabric into 1¾" sashing strips and cut into lengths as follows:

    2 strips 69¼" long
    2 strips 58" long
    2 strips 35½"long
    2 strips 13" long
    30 strips 10½" long

Red
2 outer borders 1½" x 63½"
2 outer border 1½" x 95"
104 B petals
35 B reversed petals
120 C petals
62 D petals
62 D reversed petals

Green
23 A leaves
23 A reversed leaves

Yellow
23 E flower centers
12 F half-flower centers
4 G quarter-flower centers

Backing
Cut 6 yards into two 3-yard pieces. Seam together lengthwise.

Binding
Cut bias strips 1¼" wide for ¼" finished single fold binding.

ASSEMBLY

1. Appliqué the 23 blocks, referring to Diagram 3. Begin with 1 A leaf and 1 A reversed leaf. Then add 4 B petals, 1 B reversed petal, 4 C petals, 2 D petals and 2 D reversed petals. Last, appliqué 1 E flower center to cover bases of petals.

2. Appliqué the 12 large triangles, referring to Diagram 4. Partially appliqué 1 B and 1 B reversed petal, but do not finish until after the quilt top has been assembled, when edges of B petals will be appliquéd over the border seam. Appliqué 2 C petals, 1 D petal and 1 D reversed petal. Appliqué 1 F half-flower center to cover bases of petals.

3. Appliqué the 4 small corner triangles, referring to Diagram 5. Appliqué 1 D petal, 1 D reversed petal, 1 C petal and 1 G quarter-flower center.

4. Sew the blocks, the triangles and the 1¾" x 10½" sashing strips into diagonal rows, referring to illustration for correct placement. Note that the orientation of the flowers varies from block to block. Sew the rows and the remaining sashing strips together.

5. Sew together lengthwise the wide inner borders and the narrow outer borders. Sew the border units to the quilt top. Miter the border corners.

6. Layer quilt top, batting and backing, then baste.

7. Quilt around all appliquéd pieces. Fill remaining space with diagonals or other simple background design.

8. Bind with red.

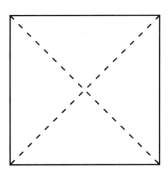

Diagram 1   Diagram 2

Diagram 3

Block Placement

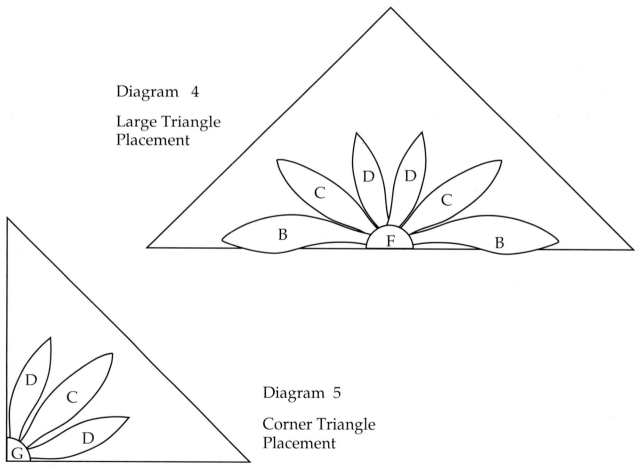

Diagram 4

Large Triangle
Placement

Diagram 5

Corner Triangle
Placement

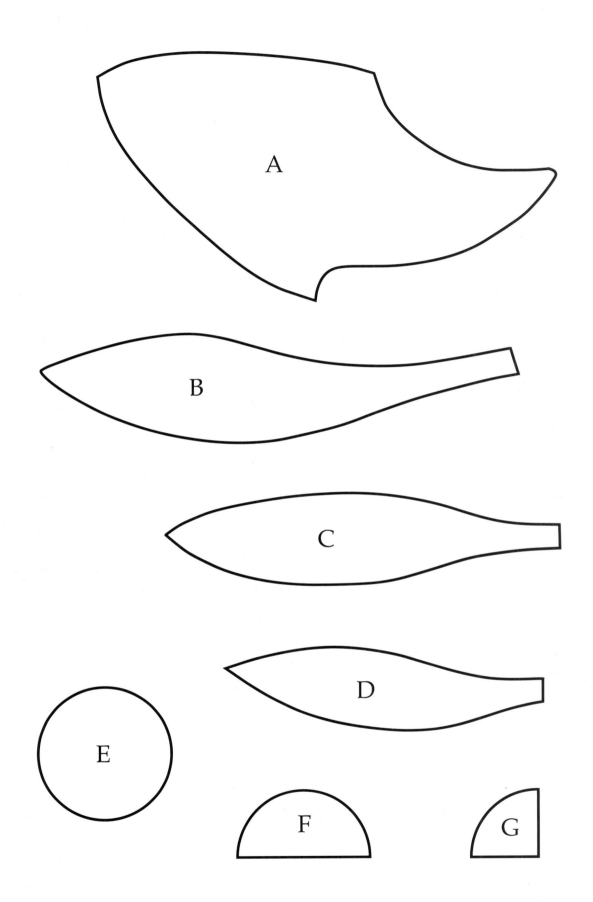

Poppy

FINISHED SIZES

Quilt: 82½" x 94"
Medallion blocks: 19½" x 25¼"
Medallion borders: each ¾" wide
Border blocks: 11½" x 19½"
Corner blocks: 12½" x 12½"
Binding: ¼" wide

YARDAGE

7½ yards white for blocks and medallion borders
3 yards green for leaves, calyxes, seed pods and stems
2 yards light pink for medallion borders, poppies,
    petals and buds
¾ yards dark pink for poppies, petals and buds
6 yards for backing
¾ yard green for binding

CUTTING

White
From 2 yards, cut
    2 medallion borders 1¼" x 44"
    2 medallion borders 1¼" x 55½"
    4 corner blocks 13" x 13"
From 5½ yards, cut
    4 medallion blocks 20" x 25¾"
    22 border blocks 12" x 20"

Light Pink
4 medallion borders 1¼" x 44"
4 medallion borders 1¼" x 55½"
22 B poppies for border blocks
4 C petals for medallion blocks
4 C reversed petals for medallion
    blocks
8 E buds for medallion blocks and
    corner blocks
4 F buds for medallion blocks
30 G buds for medallion, border and
    corner blocks

Dark Pink
4 A poppies for medallion blocks
4 A reversed poppies for medallion
    blocks
22 D petals for border blocks
8 F buds for medallion and corner
    blocks

Green
From 1 yard, cut ¾" wide bias strips
    for stems.
From 2 yards, cut
    12 J calyxes
    30 K calyxes
    30 L seed pods
    16 M leaves
    44 N leaves

Backing
Cut 6 yards into two 3-yard lengths.
Seam lengthwise.

Binding
Cut bias strips 1¼" wide for ¼"
finished single fold binding.

ASSEMBLY

1. Appliqué medallion blocks, referring to Diagram 1. Appliqué stems first, then appliqué dark pink A poppies, overlapping with light pink C petals. Note that half of the A and C pieces are reversed. Appliqué dark pink F buds, overlapping with light pink E buds and J calyxes. Appliqué light pink F buds, overlapping with J calyxes. Appliqué G buds and overlap with K calyxes. Appliqué L seed pods and M leaves.

2. Appliqué border blocks, referring to Diagram 2. First appliqué stems. Next, appliqué light pink B poppies, overlapping with dark pink D petals. Appliqué G buds and overlap with K calyxes. Appliqué L seed pods and N leaves.

3. Appliqué corner blocks, referring to Diagram 3. First appliqué stems. Next, appliqué dark pink F buds, overlapping with light pink E buds and J calyxes. Appliqué G buds, overlapping with K calyxes. Appliqué L seed pods and M leaves.

4. Piece together the 4 medallion blocks.

5. Sew a dark pink medallion border strip to either side of the white medallion border strips. Sew these units to the assembled medallion blocks and miter the corners.

6. Piece together 5 border blocks for each short side and 6 border blocks for each long side. Sew border units to medallion unit and miter the corners. Set in the corner blocks.

7. Layer quilt top, batting and backing, then baste.

8. Quilt around all appliqué pieces. In the medallion blocks, draw outlines of poppies, buds, seed pods and leaves for quilting. Fill background with diamonds or other simple design.

9. Bind with green.

Diagram 1: Medallion Block

Diagram 2: Border Block

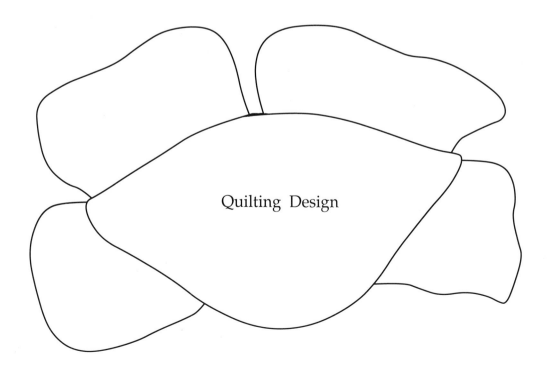

Quilting Design

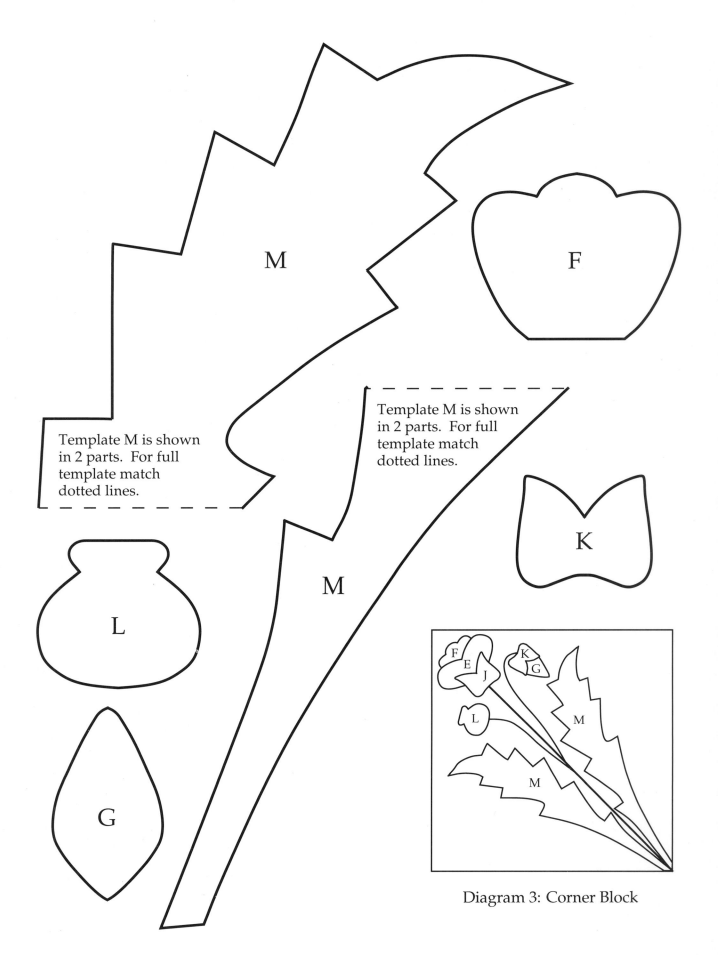

M

F

Template M is shown in 2 parts. For full template match dotted lines.

Template M is shown in 2 parts. For full template match dotted lines.

K

L

M

G

Diagram 3: Corner Block

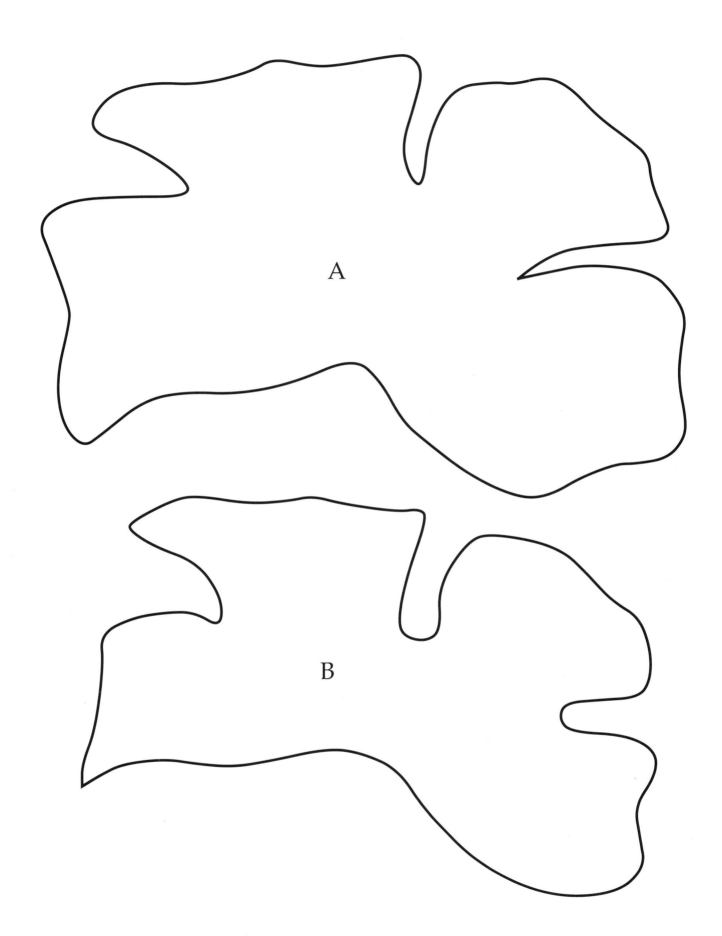

A

B

CUTTING

White
From 1¼ yards, cut center rectangle
    26½" x 36½".
From 1¼ yards, cut
    6 border pieces 1½" x 36½"
    6 border pieces 1½" x 26½"
    7 strips 1½" x 27" for corner units

Pink
8 border pieces 1½" x 36½"
8 border pieces 1½" x 26½"
7 strips 1½" x 27" for corner units

Scraps
Note: Reverse half of the pieces.
16 shoes
8 each: necks, skirts, bodices, arms,
    sleeves and hats
4 parasols and handles

Binding
Cut bias strips 1¼" wide for ¼"
finished single fold binding.

ASSEMBLY

1. Appliqué 8 lassies in facing pairs onto the center rectangle. Parasol handles and hat bands can be made from small rectangles folded in thirds lengthwise. Pieces should be layered in the following order: shoes, neck, skirt, bodice, arm, sleeve, parasol handle, hat and parasol. Lassies can be individualized by adding details to clothing, hats and parasols.

2. Sew short border pieces together to make 2 sets, consisting of 4 pink bands alternating with 3 white bands. Sew long border pieces together to make 2 sets, consisting of 4 pink bands alternating with 3 white bands.

3. Make 4 corner units, referring to Diagram 1. Sew together 7 strips, alternating 4 pink and 3 white. Sew together a second set of 7 strips with 3 pink and 4 white. Cut apart every 1½". Sew together 7 of these units for each corner unit.

4. Sew short border units to center rectangle. Sew corner units to long border units, then add to partially assembled quilt top.

5. Layer quilt top, batting and backing, then baste.

6. Quilt around all appliquéd pieces. Quilt details on skirts, hats and parasols. Quilt sunflowers, birds and picket fence on center rectangle. Complete quilting with any simple backgound design.

7. Bind with pink.

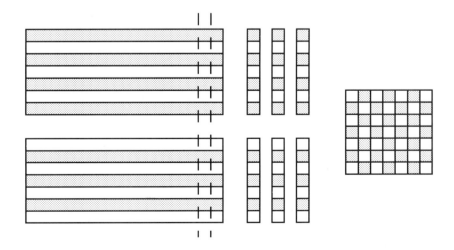

Diagram 1: Corner Units

Quilting Designs

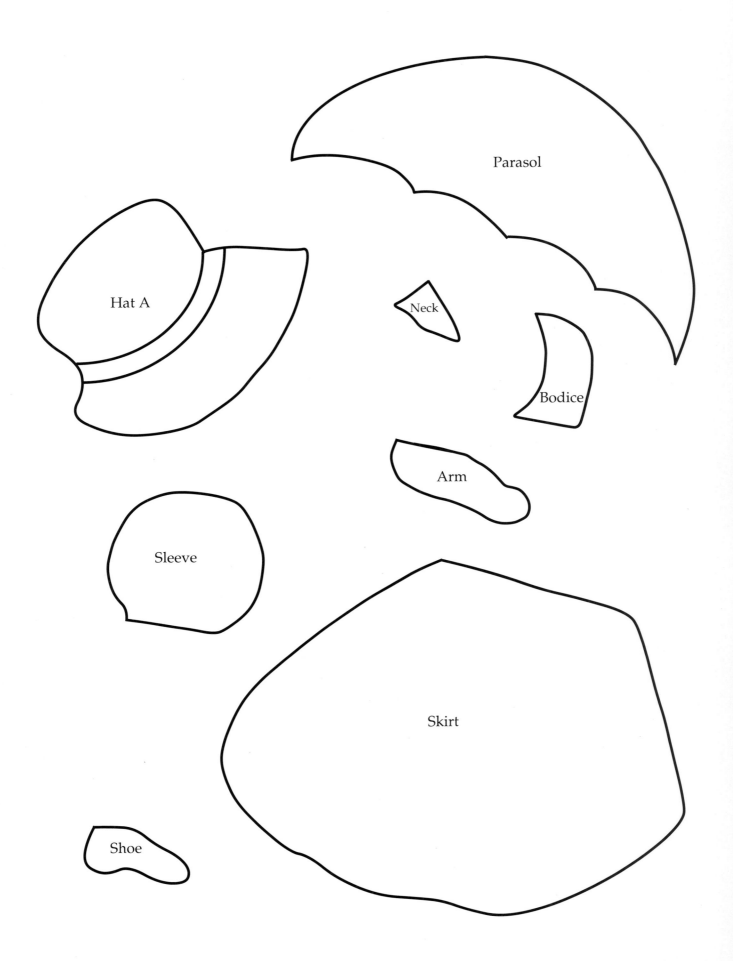

Parasol

Hat A

Neck

Bodice

Arm

Sleeve

Skirt

Shoe

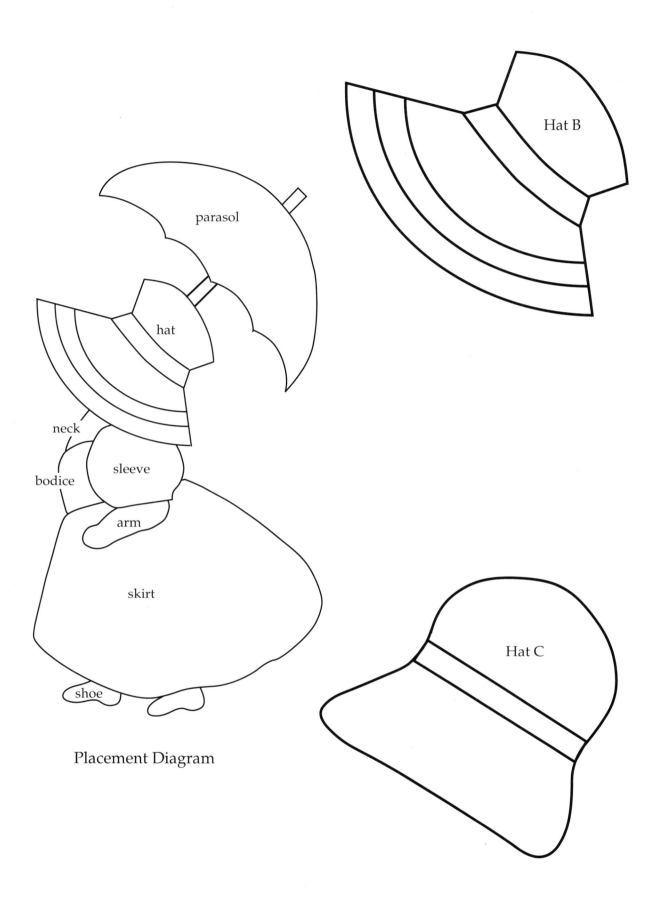

Hat B

parasol

hat

neck

bodice

sleeve

arm

skirt

shoe

Placement Diagram

Hat C

Sunflower

FINISHED SIZES

Quilt: 90" x 98"
Center block: 24" x 32"
Border blocks: 8" x 33"
Corner blocks: 33" x 33"
Waved borders: each 1" wide
Binding: 3⁄8" wide

YARDAGE

8½ yards white for blocks
4 yards green for leaves and stems
    (Two different greens may be used.)
3 yards bright yellow for flowers and border
3 yards dark yellow for flowers and border
3 yards light brown for border
½ yard dark brown for sunflower centers
9 yards for backing
1 yard dark brown for binding

Cutting

White
Center rectangle 24½" x 32½"
14 border blocks 8½" x 33½"
4 corner blocks 33½" x 33½"

Green
From ¾ yard, cut bias strips ¾" wide
　　for narrow stems.
From 3¼ yards, cut
　　14 long stems 1½" x 24½
　　8 medium stems 1¼" x 19½"
　　8 short stems 1" x 14½"
　　44 E new flower calyxes
　　16 G bud calyxes
　　36 L1 large leaves
　　38 L2 medium leaves
　　64 L3 small leaves

Bright Yellow
2 borders 2¼" x 90½"
2 borders 2¼" x 98½"
14 B1 large sunflower petals
8 B2 medium sunflower petals
8 B3 small sunflower petals
26 D new flowers
16 F buds

Dark Yellow
2 borders 2¼" x 90½"
2 borders 2¼" x 98½"
14 A1 large sunflower petals
8 A2 medium sunflower petals
8 A3 small sunflower petals
18 D new flowers

Light Brown
2 borders 2¼" x 90½"
2 borders 2¼" x 98½"

Dark Brown
14 C1 large sunflower centers
8 C2 medium sunflower centers
8 C3 small sunflower centers

Backing
Cut 9 yards into three 3-yard pieces.
Seam vertically.

Binding
Cut dark brown bias strips 1½" wide
for ⅜" finished single fold binding.

Assembly

1. Appliqué 14 border blocks, referring to Placement Diagram. First, appliqué 1½" wide stems for large sunflowers. Note that stems are placed 4" from edge of blocks to allow room for the waved borders. Appliqué remaining stems with narrow bias strips. Appliqué leaves. Partially appliqué D new flowers and overlap with E new flower calyxes. The new flowers higher on the stems are dark yellow and the new flowers lower on the stems are bright yellow. After the blocks have been assembled, finish appliquéing the new flowers over the block seams. Appliqué large sunflowers, starting with A1 petals. Overlap with B1 petals, matching the guide marks on A1 and B1. Add C1 centers last.

2. Appliqué 4 corner blocks, referring to Placement Diagram. Each corner block is made up of two medium sunflowers (A2, B2, C2), two small sunflowers (A3, B3, C3) and one group of 2 new flowers (D and E). Appliqué stems first: 1¼" wide stems for medium sunflowers and 1" wide stems for small sunflowers. Appliqué stems for buds, new flowers and leaves with narrow bias strips. Appliqué leaves, new flowers and calyxes. One new flower is only partially appliquéd at this time and completed after the blocks have been assembled. Appliqué buds and bud calyxes. Appliqué medium and small sunflowers.

3. Sew together 4 blocks for each long side and 3 blocks for each short side. Sew a corner block to each end of the 3-block units. Sew a 4-block unit to either side of the center block. Sew the three sections together. Finish appliquéing new flowers over seams.

4. Using the Border Guide, mark the 3 waved borders. Mark placement of waved borders on assembled blocks. Appliqué only the inner side of each border. Begin by appliquéing the bright yellow border. Follow with the dark yellow and then the light brown border. Baste outer edge of light brown border to quilt top.

5. Layer quilt top, batting and backing, then baste.

6. Quilt around the outside of all appliqué pieces. Quilt sunflower centers with small diamonds. Quilt spider webs and outlines of new flowers in the center block. Any background quilting design may be used in the other areas.

7. Trim all layers ¼" from marked outer edge of light brown border. Bind with dark brown.

Placement Diagram

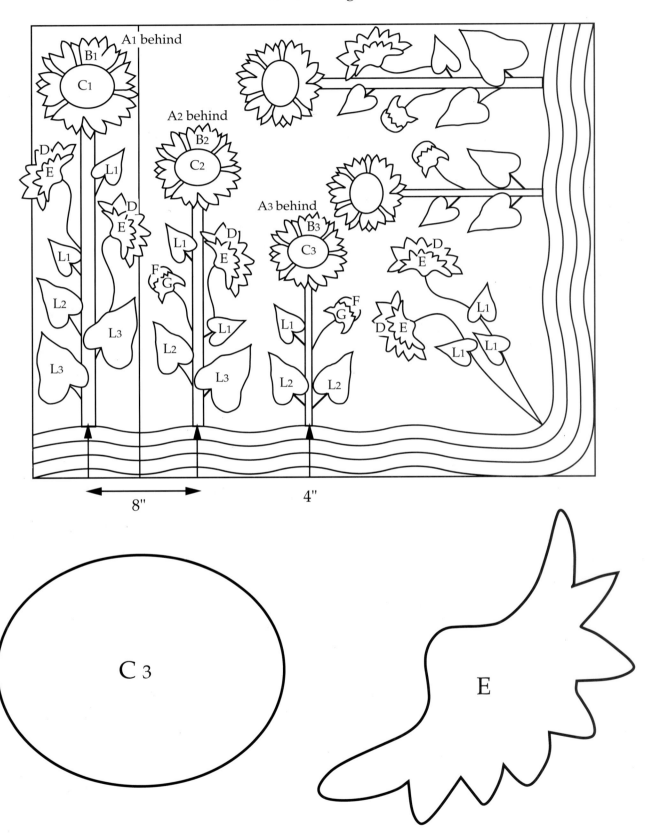

A1 behind
B1
C1

A2 behind
B2
C2

A3 behind
B3
C3

D
E
L1
L2
L3

D
E
L1
L3

F
G
L1
L2
L3

D
E
L1
L2
L2

F
G
D
E
L1
L1

8"   4"

C 3

E

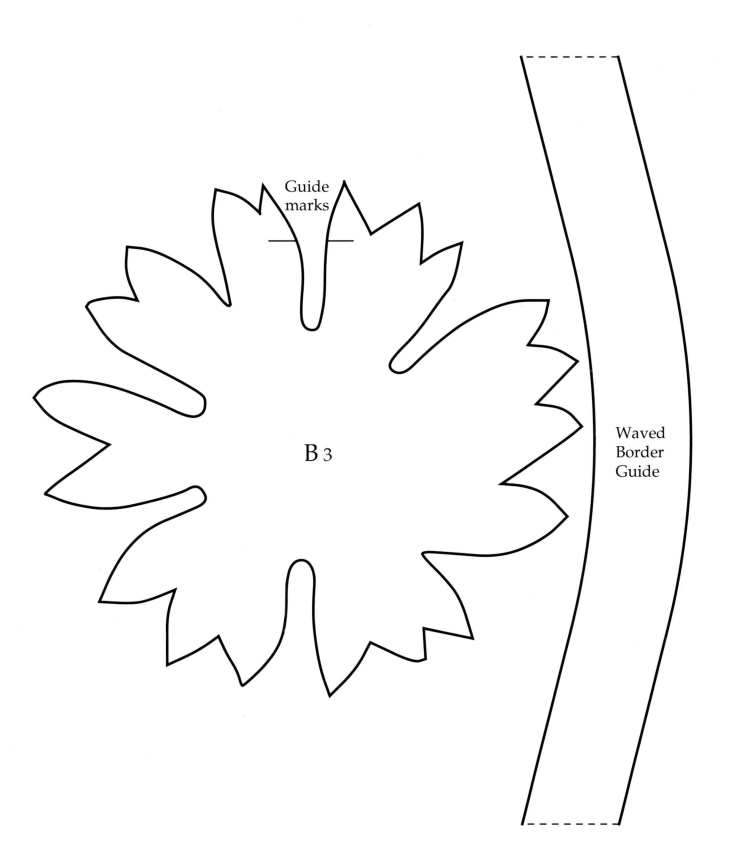

Guide
marks

B 3

Waved
Border
Guide

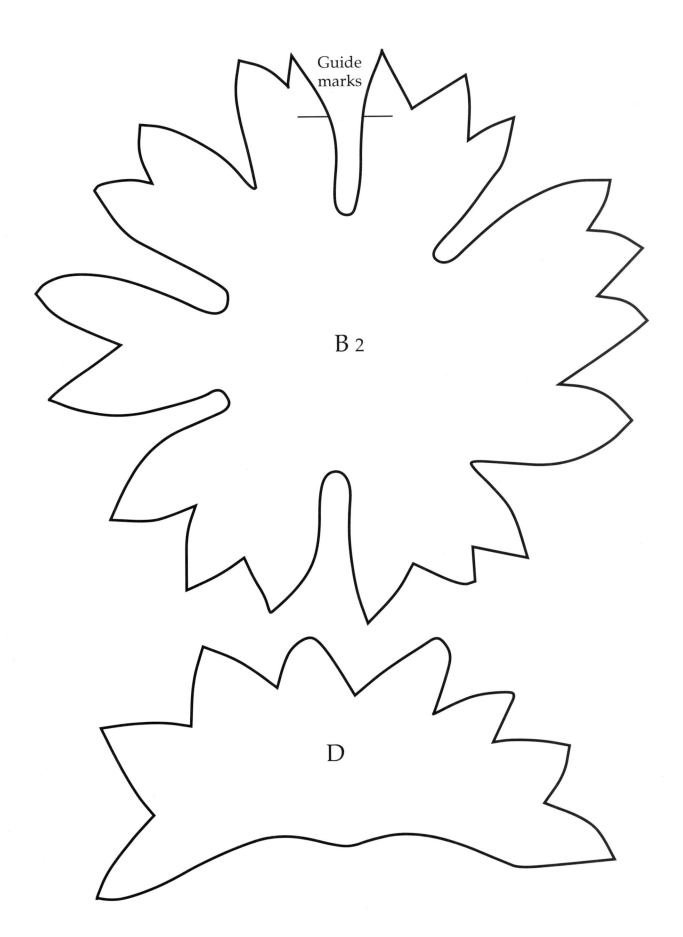

Guide marks

B 2

D

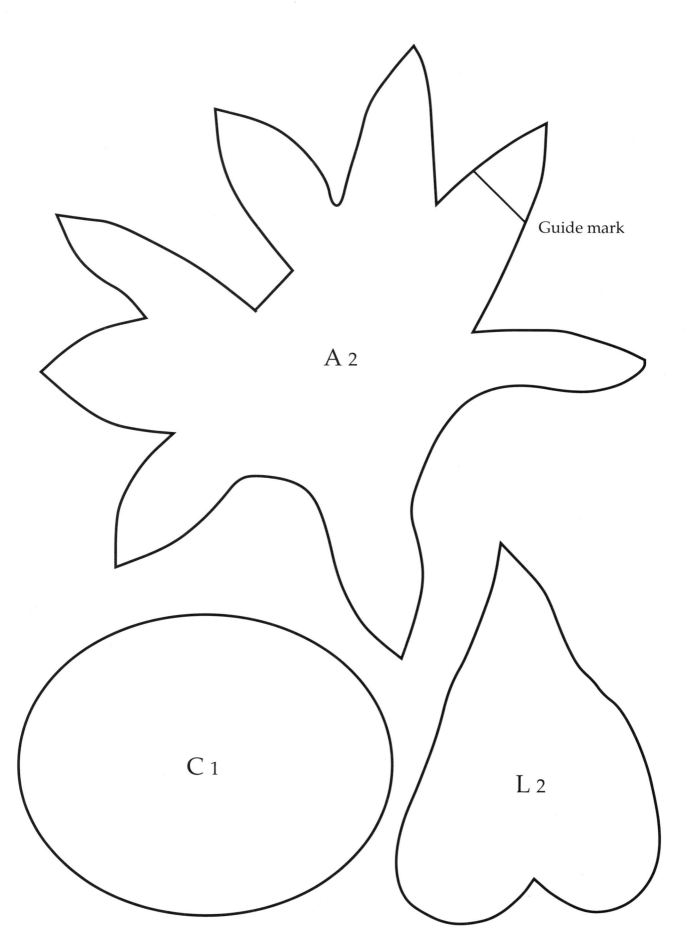

Guide mark

A 2

C 1

L 2

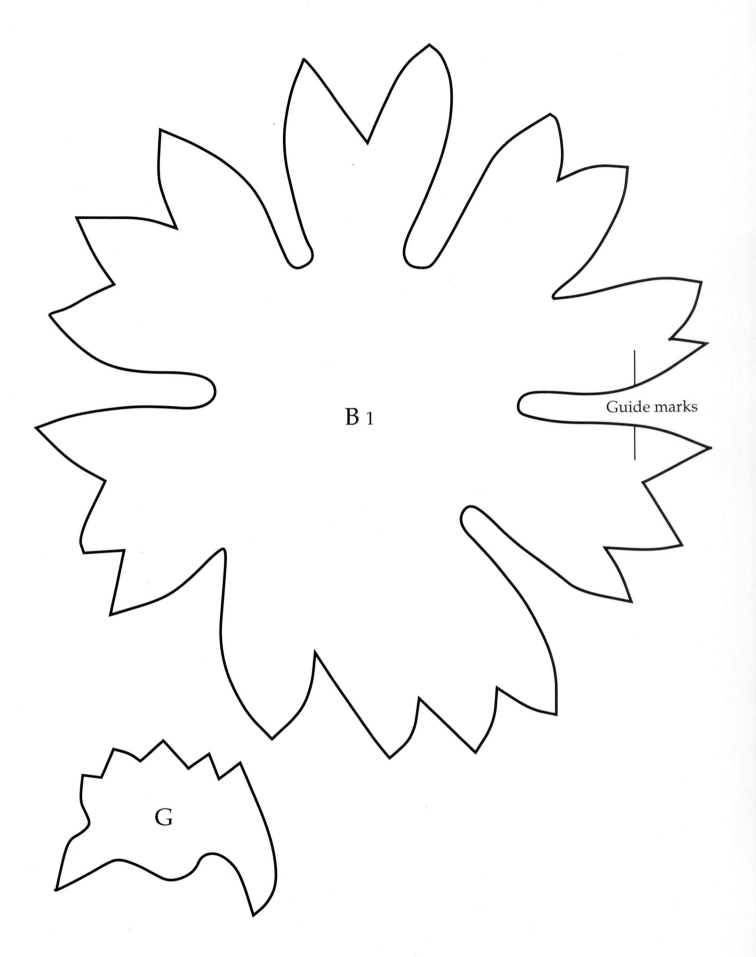

B 1

Guide marks

G

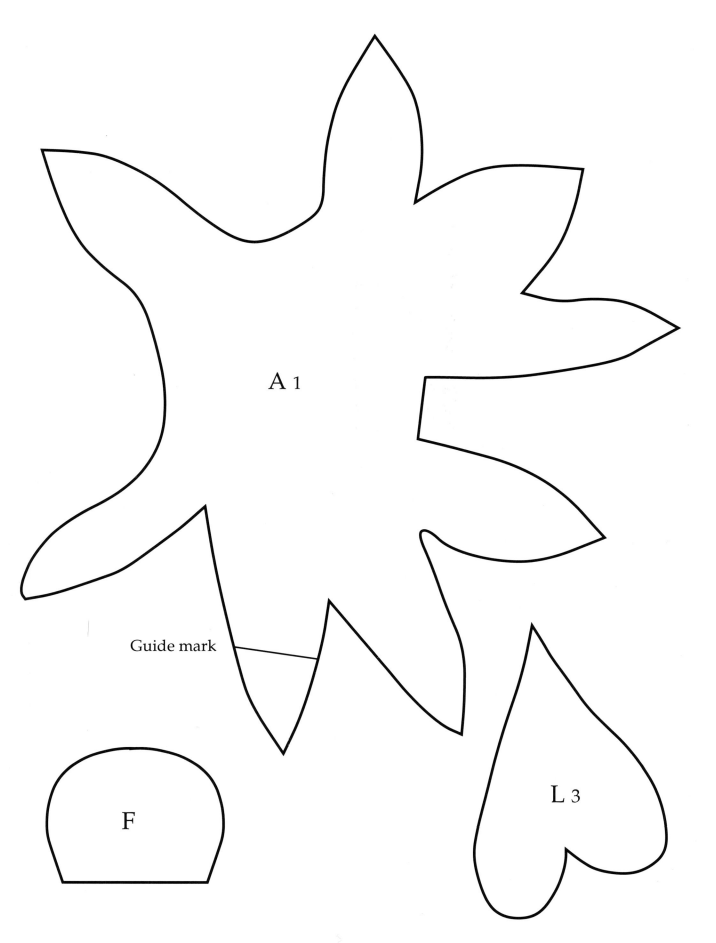

A 1

Guide mark

F

L 3

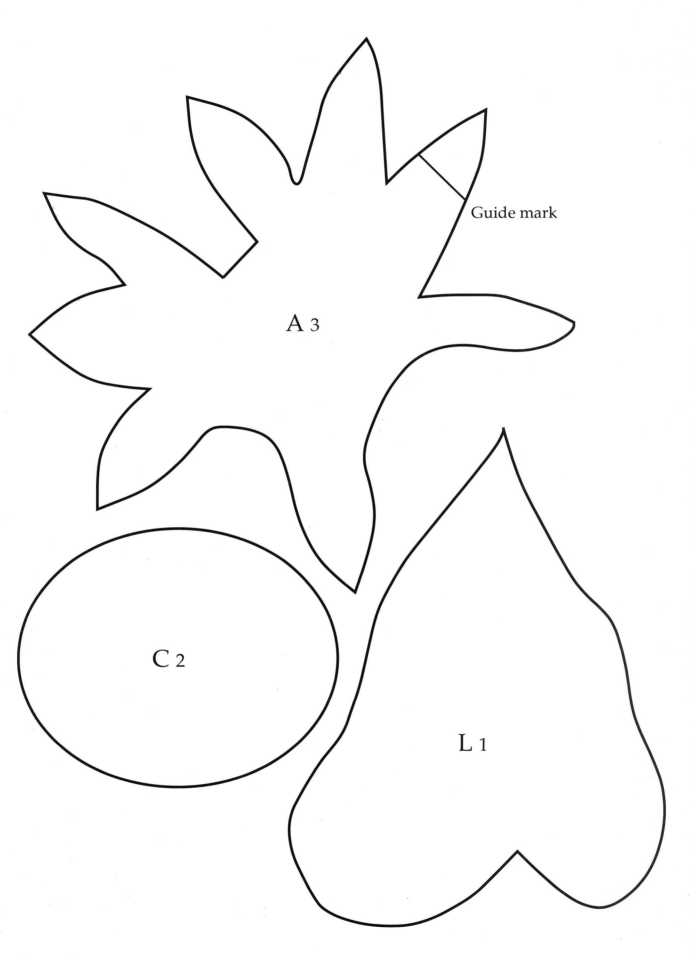

Guide mark

A 3

C 2

L 1

White Dogwood

FINISHED SIZES

Quilt: 79" x 94½"
Blocks: 11" x 11"
Binding: ¼" wide

YARDAGE

10½ yards light green for background
2 yards medium green for leaves and scalloped border
2 yards white for petals
1¼ yards brown for branches and stems
¼ yard yellow–green for flower centers
½ yard pink for petal tips
6 yards for backing
¾ yard medium green for binding

Cutting

Light Green
31 blocks 11½" x 11½"

Referring to Diagram 1, make a template for the border pentagons with dimensions as follows: long side, 15½"; short sides, 8½"; diagonals, 11". Cut 10 border pentagons, adding ¼" seam allowance on each side.

Referring to Diagram 2, make a template for the corner pentagons with dimensions as follows: long side, 24"; short sides, 8½"; diagonal, 22". Cut 4 corner pentagons, adding ¼" seam allowance on each side.

Medium Green
60 E leaves
60 E reversed leaves
36 G border scallops
4 H corner scallops

White
372 A double petals
16 B single petals

Brown
From ¾ yard, cut 18 F branches.
From ½ yard, cut bias strips ¾" wide for stems.

Yellow–green
186 D centers

Pink
760 C petal tips

Backing
Cut 6 yards into two 3-yard pieces. Seam vertically.

Binding
Cut bias strips 1¼" wide for ¼" finished single fold binding.

Assembly

1. Complete appliqué on 30 blocks. Appliqué 14 blocks as shown in Diagram 3a, 8 blocks as shown in Diagram 3b, 4 blocks as shown in Diagram 3c, and 4 blocks as shown in Diagram 3d. Note that blocks in Diagrams 3a, 3c and 3d include bias stem pieces. Begin appliqué with leaves and stems. Next appliqué the double petals, slipping the pink petal tips underneath the notches, as shown in Placement Diagram. Two double petals overlap to form a full dogwood flower. Then appliqué the single petals B and flower centers D. The center block is left plain.

2. Complete appliqué on border and corner pentagons, starting with branches and stems. Place branches 5" from the edge to allow space for scallops, as shown. Appliqué leaves, petals and flower centers.

3. Assemble blocks into diagonal rows, referring to illustration of quilt for correct placement of blocks. Sew rows together. Set in the border and corner pentagons.

4. Sew together the G and H scallops. Mark placement and then appliqué the inner edge of the scallops over the pieced border and corner pieces. Baste the outer edge of scallops to the quilt top.

5. Layer quilt top, batting and backing, then baste.

6. Quilt around all appliqué pieces. Using the dogwood blossom quilting design, quilt a wreath of flowers in the center block. Quilt blossoms in the corners of the remaining blocks. Use any simple design, such as diagonals, to fill in the remaining areas.

7. Trim layers even with the outer raw edge of the scallops. Bind with dark green.

Placement Diagram

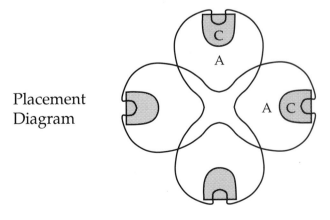

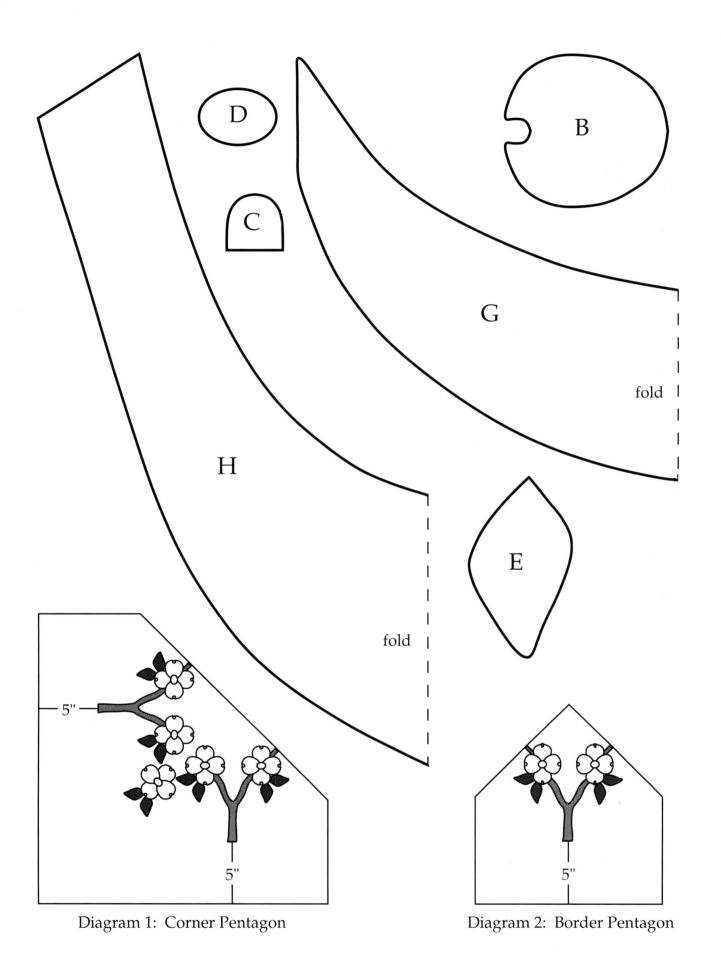

Diagram 1: Corner Pentagon

Diagram 2: Border Pentagon

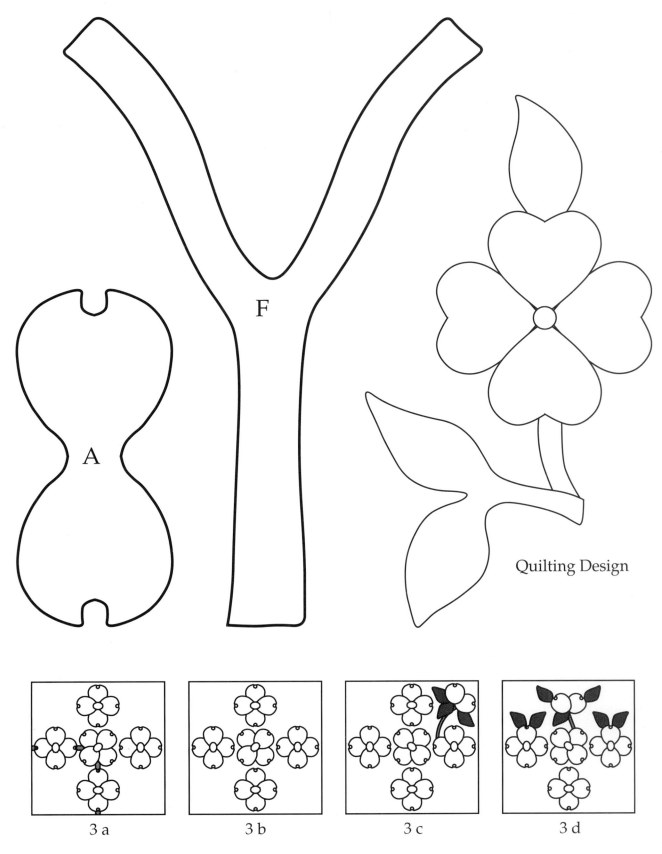

A

F

Quilting Design

3 a   3 b   3 c   3 d

Diagram 3

Suggested Reading

APPLIQUE AND QUILTING

Andreatta, Pat. *Appliqué Can Be Easy.* Warren, OH: Heirloom Stitches, 1990.

Dietrich, Mimi. *Happy Endings.* Bothell, WA: That Patchwork Place, 1987.

Leone, Diana. *Fine Hand Quilting.* Los Altos, CA: Leone Publications, 1986.

Halgrimson, Jan and Shirley Thompson. *Quilts—Start to Finish.* Edmonds, WA: St. Clair House, 1991.

McClun, Diana and Laura Nownes. *Quilts! Quilts!! Quilts!!!* San Francisco: The Quilt Digest Press, 1988.

Morris, Patricia J. *Perfecting the Quilting Stitch.* Paducah, KY: American Quilter's Society, 1990.

Sienkiewicz, Elly. *Appliqué 12 Easy Ways!* Lafayette, CA: C & T Publishing, 1991.

Simms, Ami. *How to Improve Your Quilting Stitch.* Flint, MI: Mallery Press, 1987.

MARIE WEBSTER

Benberry, Cuesta. "The 20th Century's First Quilt Revival." Part 2. *Quilter's Newsletter,* no. 115 (Sept. 1979), pp. 10–11, 37.

———. "Marie D. Webster: A Major Influence on Quilt Design in the 20th Century." *Quilter's Newsletter Magazine,* no. 224 (July/Aug. 1990), pp. 32–35.

———. "Marie Webster: Indiana's Gift to American Quilts." In *Quilts of Indiana: Crossroads of Memories.* Indiana Quilt Registry Project, Inc. Bloomington, IN: Indiana University Press, 1991.

Webster, Marie D. *Quilts: Their Story and How to Make Them.* (1915) New edition with a biography of the author by Rosalind Webster Perry. Santa Barbara, CA: Practical Patchwork, 1990.

Index

Photo Credits

The Quilters Hall of Fame

The historic Webster House in Marion, Indiana

The Quilters Hall of Fame, founded in 1979, is a non-profit organization dedicated to honoring those who have made outstanding contributions to the world of quilting.

Now, after 13 years, the Quilters Hall of Fame has found a permanent home. It will be located in Marie Webster's house in Marion, Indiana, where she lived from 1902 to 1942, designing her famous quilts and operating her successful pattern business.

After the Webster family moved away, the house fell into disrepair. Condemned as unsafe, it was recently saved from demolition by Marie's granddaughter, Rosalind Webster Perry. In 1992, the significance of the Webster House was officially recognized when it was placed on the National Register of Historic Places.

Rosalind is working with Hazel Carter, President of the Quilters Hall of Fame, to preserve the house and give it new life as a unique museum celebrating our quiltmaking heritage.

Quilters—you can be a part of quilt history! Donations are urgently needed to restore Marie Webster's home to its original condition. Help save this landmark by becoming a **Friend of the Quilters Hall of Fame**!

*To find out how **you** can join, please contact*

Rosalind Webster Perry
1009 North Ontare Road
Santa Barbara, CA 93105

Publications from Practical Patchwork

QUILTS: THEIR STORY AND HOW TO MAKE THEM

by Marie D. Webster

The 75th anniversary edition of America's first quilt book, with the complete original text and illustrations: 36 color plates, bibliography, notes and a biography of the author by Rosalind Webster Perry.

"Fans of quilt history are going to be retiring their well-thumbed copies of Marie Webster's 1915 classic Quilts *and replacing them with this new and improved edition.... We always enjoy a two-generation quilt, where a granddaughter finishes up a set of family blocks. Here we have a parallel in print. Rosalind Perry is to be congratulated on the care she has taken to carry on her grandmother's legacy."*

– Barbara Brackman, *Quilter's Newsletter Magazine*

Hardcover, $30 plus $2.50 shipping and handling.
(California residents please add sales tax.)

A JOY FOREVER: MARIE WEBSTER'S QUILT PATTERNS

by Rosalind Webster Perry and Marty Frolli

Additional copies of this book can be ordered from the publisher for $19.50 plus $2.50 shipping and handling for the first book and $1 for each additional book.
(California residents, please add sales tax.)

Send your orders to:

**PRACTICAL PATCHWORK
P.O. Box 30065
Santa Barbara, CA 93130**